WISDOM

for the Wait

WISDOM

for the Wait

by Tiffany Buckner

Anointed Fire™ House

www.AnointedFireHouse.com

Wisdom for the Wait
Copyright © 2016
Tiffany Buckner

Cover Illustration Copyright © 2016 by Anointed Fire™ House
Cover design by Anointed Fire™ House
Book design and production by Anointed Fire™ House
(www.anointedfirehouse.com)

Anointed Fire
info@anointedfire.com
www.anointedfirehouse.com

Ordering Information:
Quantity sales. Special discounts are available on quantity purchases by corporations, associations, and others. For details, contact the publisher at the email address above.
Orders by U.S. trade bookstores and wholesalers.

This book is designed to provide information and motivation to our readers. It is sold with the understanding that the publisher is not engaged to render any type of psychological, legal, or any other kind of professional advice. No warranties or guarantees are expressed or implied by the author, since every man has his own measure of faith. The individual author(s) shall not be liable for any physical, psychological, emotional, financial, or commercial damages, including; but not limited to, special, incidental, consequential or other damages. Our views and rights are the same: You are responsible for your own choices, actions, and results.

All scriptures noted in this book were taken from the King James Bible, English Standard Version, New Living Translation and New International Version unless otherwise noted.

ISBN-13: 978-0692693704

ISBN-10: 069269370X

I dedicate this book to the many women who have chosen to honor God by waiting for their God-appointed spouses. You are a rare breed and you are definitely blessed.

TABLE OF CONTENTS

Introduction

Wisdom for the Wait is an engaging self help guide for the women who choose to wait on God for their husbands. This book is designed to encourage and exhort the women of God and to help them to see their seasons of singleness for what they are— seasons of change and seasons of preparation.

In this powerful book, you will come to understand the reason for the wait. In addition to this, you will better understand the purpose of abstinence and the process that we must undergo to be made ready for our husbands.

Why Do We Wait?

In the United States, no sane and healthy woman absolutely has to be single, regardless of how many children she has, how she looks, how much money she makes, how good or bad her family is, etc. A single woman in the States is oftentimes single by choice. We choose to be in a relationship when we come across people we believe to be compatible with us and we choose to be single when we don't come across such souls. At the same time, many single Christian women opt to be single because they want their God-ordained husbands, rather than just some random man who has a handsome face and a few good qualities.

I am a single woman in the Lord who is happily and patiently waiting for her God-appointed husband. I learned from my mistakes, and I have learned who I am in Christ Jesus, even though much of my identity is still being revealed to me. Like most women, I have had guys who were interested in pursuing a relationship with me, but I declined their offers because I knew that they weren't the ones God had purposed for me. How did I know this? By simply knowing God and knowing myself.

The more you learn about God, the more of His traits you will look for when a man starts displaying any type of romantic interest in you. If the man is profane, secular and sexually immoral, you will automatically know that he is not the one God sent. How so? He is nothing like God, and we know that God won't send someone who is not submitted to Him to pursue any of His daughters. After all, we are told to submit to our husbands. A woman who marries an ungodly man has the same charge; she has to submit to her husband, but of course, she does not have to submit to his demons. This means that she will have to learn to discern between her husband's petitions versus the evil petitions of the enemy. We wait so that we don't end up with men like this. We wait because we trust God and we want His best for us. Lastly, we wait because we understand that we are more than just wives; we are purpose-filled creatures who are in the realm of the earth on an assignment by God. The wrong men could easily take us off course and cause us to fail these assignments.

Waiting for the God-appointed husband is not an easy task, but it's not supposed to be easy. That's because anything that requires faith requires that we give up our own habits and thinking patterns to trust in the promises of God. Faith opposes the nature of our flesh and the nature of our flesh opposes faith. I've come to believe that the wait itself is one of God's ways of building our faith. After all, it is during these waits that we are oftentimes presented with some unique, once-in-a-lifetime opportunities to have the relationships and the things we once dreamed of having. However, we have to turn down these opportunities to demonstrate our faith in God and the unyielding perseverance we have to please Him.

It wasn't long ago when one of my exes reached out to me. Truthfully, I can't say that he was really an ex (per-se), but more-so, he was a former lover of mine. I was only 18 years old when I met Ivan and he was eight years my senior. My brother introduced me to Ivan, and for whatever reason, the two of us seemed to hit it off almost immediately.

At the time, Ivan was in a relationship with

a woman and the two of them had a child together. I've never been the type of woman who desired to "take" some woman's man because I knew I couldn't trust him, but during that dark stage of my life, I did like the attention I got from single and married men alike. I was a broken creature who looked for love and validation in the eyes of men.

My initial relationship with Ivan was a friendly one. He was a great listener, and I loved to hear his stories of faith and perseverance. He had been through a lot and had overcome a lot—as a young woman, his stories fascinated and wowed me. Nevertheless, I wasn't really romantically interested in Ivan. There was an attraction there—I admit that, but the attraction wasn't one that made me want to marry the guy. Our attraction to one another was sexual, and of course, there was somewhat of a romantic curiosity present as well. I loved the way Ivan looked at me and how he made me feel. I knew that he was very attracted to me and I used this to my advantage. I would flirt with him, and I would even tease him by wearing revealing clothing, but I did not want to have an affair with him. Howbeit, all of the flirting and teasing eventually led to an affair, and I found myself wearing a label that had always been repulsive to me —I was the other woman.

Even though I was Ivan's mistress of sorts, I excused my behavior by reminding myself that Ivan wasn't married to his girlfriend, plus, I had no intentions in "taking" him. In my youthful ignorance, I was just having fun. Nevertheless, that fun would end when I had a pregnancy scare. The fear of becoming a mother was enough to wake me up from my stupor. Not only would having a child take away my freedom, but I would end up having a child with a man who I couldn't see a future with. I knew I couldn't trust Ivan, so I hadn't considered having a future with him; the thought had never crossed my mind. And to make matters worse, Ivan was a little too excited about the idea of me being pregnant and this told me that he was getting too serious about me. I was terrified and when I found out that I was not pregnant, I immediately ended things with Ivan.

Now, here it was twenty years later and he had found me yet again. He reached out to me on Facebook, told me that he was divorced and that he had never stopped thinking about me. By this time, I was a woman after God's heart and I was waiting for my God-appointed husband. I was completely a new creature in Christ, so even though he had found Tiffany in the flesh, he hadn't found the immoral, self-seeking, lost and perverse woman I once was. I had to take into consideration that

Ivan could possibly be "the one," especially given the fact that he had somewhat matched a prophecy that I had received about my husband. I laughed at the idea of Ivan being my husband. If people asked us how we met, what could I say?

Ivan had changed a lot as well. Of course, it was twenty years later and he'd obviously matured, but I didn't stick around to truly get to know him. After our first conversation, it was easy for me to conclude that he was not my appointed man of God. He wasn't in the Lord, even though he claimed to believe in Him and serve Him in his own unique way.

Ivan had done well for himself career-wise, and he seemed to know what he wanted romantically as well. At this point, I could see a future with him, but that future didn't look bright. Ivan represented what was familiar to me. Even though I knew that if I stuck around, we would end up married with children, I also knew that I would be going back down the same paths I had once taken. I would be marrying another man who wasn't in the Lord and I would likely end up in divorce court yet again. The most telling part was that Ivan himself was going through a divorce, which meant he was still married. Again, it was that first conversation that told me everything I needed to know. I ended up talking with Ivan for a total of three days before the Lord rebuked me. Any time spent entertaining Ivan was time wasted and blessings delayed. At the same time, even though Ivan and I hadn't seen one another physically, the time I spent talking with him could have easily led us both into an emotional soul tie. I ended all of my communications with Ivan, and I decided to continue waiting for my God-assigned husband.

Why did I share this story? I shared this story to demonstrate a point—waiting is a choice; it's intentional. I didn't have to wait, but <u>I chose</u> to wait on God because <u>I believe</u> that He has better in store for me. I choose to continue waiting until God sends the one He has specifically assigned to my life because I know that my assignment in Christ Jesus is linked to my God-ordained marriage. Choosing the wrong man is a selfish act; it's the same as disregarding the fact that you are a creature of purpose. It's what we believe about God and what we believe about ourselves that will determine if we are willing to wait and if we are willing to reject the wrong men, even if they appear to be near-perfect matches for our lives.

Ivan and I had a history together, even though that history was pretty seedy. Ivan and I both wanted to be loved, married and have faithful spouses; for some, this would have been enough. For me, my faith in God won't let me settle, and even though some people may not understand why I choose to wait, I can rest assured that I'm making the right choice. I choose to wait because I choose faith over chance. I've gambled a lot in relationships and I found out the hard way that you can never take chances with your soul and win. In order to please God, we have to have faith in Him and do things that most people will not and cannot understand. We have to be made to look like fools in order for us to allow God to get the glory from our lives. Are you willing to wait? That's a question that only you can answer, but your answer will determine your harvest.

Hebrews 11:6 (NIV): "And without faith it is impossible to please God, because anyone who comes to him must believe that he exists and that he rewards those who earnestly seek him."

What are You Waiting for?

An important question to ask yourself is: *What am I waiting for?* Your answer will determine how long you are willing to wait and whether or not your wait is driven by the right things or the wrong motives. One of the things I've noticed with some waiting women is that their motives aren't right, so their waiting isn't inspired by their desires to serve God. Their waits are nothing more than another tool that they're using in their attempts to manipulate Heaven and force God to give them the husbands they have been praying for.

Let's face it. We aren't perfect creatures, and if we perform daily heart-checks, one of the things we'll notice is that we have tried to manipulate God at some point or another. We told Him what He wanted to hear, hoping that our words would move Him to give us whatever it was we were asking for. We've obeyed Him from time-to-time, hoping that our obedience would cause Him to favor us and give us the desires of our hearts. Nevertheless, our tools of manipulation were destroyed as we got closer to God and began to understand Him all the more. We came to understand that not only is He a faithful and good God; He is also all-knowing, which means that He knows everything. Nothing is hidden from Him, not even the motives of our hearts.

One of the most common pits I've seen mature Christian women fall into is what I refer to as Jezebel's snare. In this, the believer comes to a point in her wait where she begins to get anxious and this anxiousness causes her to question God. She questions whether God has truly chosen her husband for her or if the idea of

having a God-ordained husband is nothing
more than religious, romantic heresy. She
reasons within herself that we are choice-
driven creatures given to will and that God
does not infringe upon our will. She
reasons within herself that some women
have gone out and chosen their own guys,
and thirty years later, they are still married
to those guys. Truthfully, this is a
transitional point; this is where those
whose motives are wrong will begin to
faint, while those who have pure motives
are tested and proven. Howbeit, the
woman whose motives are impure will
give up waiting and she will go out and
choose her own guy. But here's the issue.
Not only will she choose her own guy, but
she will then try to pass him off as her God-
appointed husband. In other words, she
will attempt to lead other women astray
because she doesn't want them to be found
by their God-appointed husbands. After
all, this would not only be humiliating to

her, but it would serve as confirmation to her that she failed at waiting. Because of this, she will begin to minister to women in her attempts to get them to fall into the same snares she's fallen into. Believe it or not, women like this will always be successful at leading other women astray because there will always be women out there who are more interested in being wives than they are in pleasing the Lord. After all, their waits were driven by selfish ambition and not their love for God.

I've seen women holding conferences where they are literally teaching women how to find their own husbands. Some of them even get bold enough to tell the women that if they follow their advice, they will have their husbands within a specific time-frame. Of course, this is an attempt to mock God and the women who head up these movements against righteousness are doing so because this is their way of trying to validate their own relationships. At the same time, unbeknownst to them, they are attempting to discredit God by teaching women to "perform" acts and rituals to draw husbands to themselves, rather than just believing God and trusting that He will send their husbands to them in due season. In other words, you can't put a time-frame on when God moves and you definitely can't force Him to move any faster; you can only obey Him, stay in His will and trust Him. In due season, you will reap whatever it is that you have sown if you don't give up.

Ecclesiastes 3:1-8 (ESV): "For everything there is a season, and a time for every matter under heaven: a time to be born, and a time to die; a time to plant, and a time to pluck up what is planted; a time to kill, and a time to heal; a time to break down, and a time to build up; a time to weep, and a time to laugh; a time to mourn, and a time to dance; a time to cast away stones, and a time to gather stones together; a time to embrace, and a time to refrain from embracing; a time to seek, and a time to lose; a time to keep, and a time to cast away; a time to tear, and a time to sew; a time to keep silence, and a time to speak; a time to love, and a time to hate; a time for war, and a time for peace."

Galatians 6:9 (ESV): "And let us not grow weary of doing good, for in due season we will reap, if we do not give up."

Proverbs 19:21 (NLT): "You can make many plans, but the Lord's purpose will prevail."

What I've found is that we all have a destination that we're trying to get to; it is the very peak of our desires. For example, some women desire to be married, have children and be happy; this is the full extent of their desires. This means that having a husband and children is their peak. Many of these women will try to

spice up "their" plans with a few Christian
words and a few charitable works, but God
knows the depths and secrets of our hearts.
He knows what it is that we desire the
most. That's why He told us to seek first the
kingdom of God and all His righteousness,
and by doing so, He would add everything
else to us (see Matthew 6:33). Pleasing the
Lord, bringing others to Christ and
inheriting the kingdom of God should be
our greatest desires, but to get to this point,
we have to study the Word and get to
know God better. That's why He said that
we ought to taste and see that He is good
(see Psalm 34:8). This is the point that God
is trying to get every single Christian
woman to, because if you do not seek God
first, you will make an idol out of yourself,
your husband, and your
marriage—guaranteed. You see, when you
seek God more than you seek anything
else, you will put God before anything and
anyone else. God wants to demonstrate

how good He is to us, but we have to be willing to put Him first and let Him take the lead in our lives.

There was a time when my greatest desire was to be married with children, happy, financially stable and Heaven-bound. Such thinking was the evidence of my immaturity because I was self-seeking and I put God in the backseat of my desires. Of course, God will not accept any other place than the driver's seat of our lives, therefore, when we attempt to give Him any other place, He simply washes His hands and lets us chase our dreams—alone.

Wrongful thinking led me into two failed marriages and a whole lot of heartache, but I decided to stop chasing the pleasures of life; I decided to seek the kingdom of God. It was that change of heart that made it easy for me to reject Ivan and any other man who could have helped me to live the life I once wanted. Nowadays, my dreams aren't wrapped in the flesh; I simply desire to please the Lord. Now, don't get me wrong—I still want to be happily married with children, and I still desire to be financially stable and Heaven-bound, but those desires are no longer my "peak desires." They are simply add-ons. My greatest desire these days is to please God, win souls for the kingdom of God, advance the kingdom of God in the realm of the earth, serve God by serving His people, etc. In other words, I am no longer self-absorbed. My desires no longer peak at me getting what I want; the pinnacle of my success is in winning souls for Christ.

You have to ask yourself what it is that you want the most, and then, you have to do one of the hardest things known to mankind— you have to be honest with yourself. It is so easy to operate in false humility and say the things that we know

God wants to hear because we've trained ourselves to become religious parakeets who say the right things, all the while, harboring not-so-godly motives.

Matthew 15:8 (NIV): "These people honor me with their lips, but their hearts are far from me."

What exactly are you waiting for? Is your happiness your greatest desire? If so, don't beat yourself up; simply repent and ask the Lord to give you a heart after His own heart. Understand this about God— He will never release a man to cover and lead you if that man doesn't have a heart after His own heart, and at the same time, you will never attract such a man if you don't have the heart of God.

Jeremiah 3:15 (ESV): "And I will give you shepherds after my own heart, who will feed you with knowledge and understanding."

Let pleasing God be your greatest desire. Don't let your imaginations, voids and desires lead you into idolatry. Seek God above all things and it is then and only then that He will hide you so that your husband can find you. A woman who has not been hidden by God cannot be found by her God-appointed husband, regardless of how well she tries to hide.

Manipulating the Wait

In the previous chapter, I mentioned Jezebel's snare, whereas, many believing women come to a point in their waits that they begin to question their waits. They question whether they are waiting in vain and if they've somehow allowed the concept of there being one man who God has designed for them to rob them of the opportunity to get married. Truthfully, every woman comes to this point in her wait; it is nothing but a test of our faith, and it will always separate the women with the wrong motives from the ones who have pure motives.

I can't tell you how many times I've come across believing women who have gotten into relationships with the wrong men and tried to pass those guys off as their God-appointed husbands. Sometimes, I truthfully wonder if they sincerely think they are deceiving God or if they themselves are so deceived that they cannot see the truth. One of the most common deceptions I've witnessed is this: Some woman meets a man who is NOT practicing purity. He is not in submission to God, or in some cases, he is not in full submission to God. The women then take the lead and tell their new guys that they themselves practice purity and would continue to do so until marriage. Their new guys agree to "their terms" (not God's Word) and they continue to engage in these unequally yoked relationships. The women then try to pass off these guys as their God-appointed husbands, but in truth, these men are nothing more than their "fall-off" points. These were the guys who found them when they were ready to give up on God or they had given up on God. Nevertheless, because these women value their places in their local churches, communities or in their own ministries, they continue to portray themselves as women who have completed their waits God's way. They then pass off their non-submitted lovers as men of God before handing the mic to these men to help them mislead God's daughters into godless marriages, and sometimes, sexual immorality.

Such women end up operating as Jezebels in their marriages because they have to lead their husbands to Christ, and all too often, their guys aren't all that interested in following the Lord. They pursued the women; that's the extent or peak of their desires with her. Nevertheless, the women still desire to have their God-appointed husbands, or at least, have men who appear to be their God-appointed husbands. These women are manipulating the wait because their motives are ungodly;

they want marriage more than they want God. They will never admit to this, but the truth is in their actions, and not-so-much their words.

Matthew 7:16 (ESV): "By their fruit you will recognize them. Are grapes gathered from thornbushes, or figs from thistles?"

As a minister of the Lord who promotes purity and teaches women to wait for their husbands, I've had quite a few women with wrong motives reach out to me. They wanted to ally their ministries with my own because, again, their motives weren't right. They want validation so they can continue to convince themselves that they are in God's will and to convince others that their words are from Heaven. But, I refuse to ally myself with such souls because it reminds me of Jehoshaphat's alliance to Ahab and Jezebel and his alliance with King Ahaziah. Those alliances got him in a lot of trouble with God.

2 Chronicles 19:1-3 (ESV): "Jehoshaphat the king of Judah returned in safety to his house in Jerusalem. But Jehu the son of Hanani the seer went out to meet him and said to King Jehoshaphat, 'Should you help the wicked and love those who hate the LORD? Because of this, wrath has gone out against you from the LORD. Nevertheless, some good is found in you, for you destroyed the Asheroth out of the land, and have set your heart to seek God.'"

2 Chronicles 20:37 (ESV): "Then Eliezer the son of Dodavahu of Mareshah prophesied against Jehoshaphat, saying, 'Because you have joined with Ahaziah, the LORD will destroy what you have made.' And the ships were wrecked and were not able to go to Tarshish."

Again, I can't co-sign on anything that goes against the instructions that God has given us through His Word. He told us to not be unequally yoked with unbelievers (see 2

Corinthians 6:14). Believe it or not, this includes the unbelievers who frequent church.

There are more women attempting to manipulate waiting than those who are genuinely waiting on God for their appointed husbands. The reason for this, again, is the wait requires a level of faith that many of us do not have. This means that we need to build on our faith, and truthfully, there aren't many women who are willing to do this. The reason for this is because faith challenges the very nature of our flesh, motives and our lives as a whole. Most people aren't willing to give up their idols to follow God and that's the not-so-popular truth. Because of this, many try to manipulate the wait by:

- Pretending to be abstinent, when in truth, they are having sex or they are masturbating.
- Practicing abstinence as a tool to

manipulate some man into marrying them. Abstinence is our Romans 12:1 sacrifice; it is an offering of love and should never be used as a tool of manipulation.

- Practicing abstinence for the sole sake of petitioning God to send them husbands. When a woman's motives are wrong, she ends up having a very extensive wait because God is waiting for her to give herself to Him. Such women re-enter fornication when they see their friends and family members getting married to men they've fornicated with. In other words, having a husband is their "peak" or their greatest desires, so when their attempts to manipulate God are unfruitful, they return to their sins.

- Pretending to be waiting on the God-appointed spouse, when, in truth, they are simply playing a game of "let's make a deal" with Satan. Simply put, many women are tired of the "types" of guys that the enemy keeps sending their way, so their pursuit of God and their declarations of purity are nothing more than them protesting their own god: Satan. Once Satan gives in and sends them what appears to be a better man, they end their protests and re-enter fornication. This is what I call a celibate fornicator, or better yet, a fornicator holding a picket sign.

- Pretending to wait because they want to disprove the theory of waiting on God for a husband. You'd be amazed at how many women are obeying God for the sake of disproving Him or His teachings. Like the Pharisees of old, they test God and their goal is to have some experience to back up their claims that waiting for God and abstaining from premarital sex are both fruitless, religious gestures designed by churches to manipulate and control women. Of course, God won't send a husband to such a soul; instead, she oftentimes finds herself reaping a man who reflects the evil nature of her own heart. When this happens and she thinks she's gotten a good man, she will support the Word of God and validate God's leaders, but when the true nature of her beau is on display, she will return to her initial goal of trying to discredit the Word of God, or at least, redefine it.

Women who manipulate their waits are under the influence of the Jezebel spirit and some of them have even submitted to (or been led by) the Jezebel spirit. It is a ruling power in their lives and because spirits have personalities, such women take on the personalities of the spirits that are leading them. They want to be married more than anything; marriage has become their idol. However, they don't want to be godly wives who submit to their husbands, even though many will claim that they do. They want men who follow their leads— men who give them the desires of their wicked hearts. Many of these women are still soul tied to men from their pasts and they haven't forgiven their past lovers, so their new relationships are nothing more than extensions of their past relationships. It's basically like telling the same story with a different leading man.

We have to always check our motives to ensure that they are not only pure, but that our greatest desire is to give God the glory. Our plans should never be centered around ourselves. If we continue in our pursuits of selfish gain, we will always find ourselves under the influence (or control) of the

Jezebel spirit, and we will manipulate our waits. Women who do this end up with many stories of betrayal, deceit, lust, and pain and they only get more bitter and more manipulative in time. Seek God over a man and God will lead your husband to you. Your husband will find you in the will of God, prepared to be his wife and more than anything, he will find you already content with the life you have.

The Truth About Abstinence

I was still young in the faith when I started
going through my first divorce. I loved
God and I was determined to please Him
with my life, so I declared to myself and
one of my closest friends that I would
remain abstinent until I was married again.
My divorce wasn't yet finalized and I was
living alone for the first time in my life.
Being of little faith, I found myself trying to
heal myself, deal with my newfound
loneliness and battle the humiliation I was
feeling by surrounding myself with people.
It didn't matter where they were in the
Lord or if they were in the Lord, I just
wanted someone around me because I had
too much going on in my mind and I
wanted to silence that activity.

One of my friends was going through a

divorce as well, and we decided to act as accountability partners for one another. We both wanted to practice abstinence and do things God's way. But what I didn't realize was that abstinence is way more than not having sex; it is a mindset. Because I didn't realize this, I put myself in situations where I was tempted. On one occasion, I allowed a guy to invite himself over to my house, but when the time came for him to come over, he called and wanted to know what we were going to do. I proudly stood my ground, notifying him that I was abstinent and would remain that way until I was remarried. (Mind you, I was still married because my divorce wasn't final.) After a brief pause, he began to echo my words, trying to see if I was saying what he thought I was saying. After I confirmed this, he said he would be by the house at seven-thirty that evening. After disconnecting the line, I laughed and called my accountability partner. We both laughed at the incident because we knew that he was not coming to my house. I felt great. My first would-be relationship had ended before it could start, and it was all because I stood my ground. I bragged about the incident for a while, but I didn't realize that Satan had another trick up his sleeve.

Months later, I met another guy and I was more than happy to tell him that I was abstinent and would remain that way until marriage and he responded favorably. He told me that he was Christian, and he would respect my stance. I wanted things to go back to what I considered to be normal. I wanted to be married and planning a family with my husband. Being married was what I was accustomed to, so not only was it unwise for me to court while married, but it was unwise for me to try to court someone when I was still soul tied with my ex. When we do this, we often try to resurrect our old lives, only with new people.

My new friend would come by my house often. It felt great to have someone to cook for once again, so anytime he announced that he would be stopping by, I'd run to the store to get something to cook. I wanted to show him that I was wife material, even though I wasn't too interested in having him for my husband. I was just lonely and trying to recapture that feeling of "normal" that I'd lost when I separated from my ex. In other words, I didn't know how to be alone. Again, this is normal for a newly separated man or woman.

After he arrived at my place, I would turn on a movie, grab him a plate of whatever I cooked, and we would sit on opposite ends of the couch watching television. My accountability partner was livid. She constantly rebuked me for allowing my guy to stop by the house, but having little knowledge about purity, I would always tell her that nothing happened and nothing was going to happen between me and my guy. I was telling the truth—nothing had happened, but that didn't mean it wouldn't happen. The guy I was seeing (we'll call him Clyde) was coming by the house for more than a month, and he seemed okay with the arrangement. He had never made a move on me and he spent a few nights sleeping at the other end of my sectional couch. I thought this behavior was adorable. Here were two people trying to have a relationship, sleeping on opposite ends of the couch and there was no sex or kisses involved. Once again, I felt great. I thought I had abstinence down-packed.

One night, Clyde came to the house at his usual time to watch television with me and eat a little supper. I'd cooked chicken dressing and made a pecan pie. Of course, I was only trying to impress him. We began watching a movie, and after we finished eating, we took our plates into the kitchen and returned to the den to finish up the movie. Again, we always sat on opposite ends of my sectional sofa. The living room was dark and the movie was playing when I heard Clyde say something to the effect of, "You know, I come over here all the time, and you never sit close to me. I know your feelings about abstinence. I'm not going to disrespect you. I know that you are a woman of God. I see you over there flinching, and I just want you to sit close to me so I can wrap my arms around you." I continued to stare at the television screen, but my thoughts were racing. Would it be safe for me to sit close to him? Again, I thought that I could control the situation. After all, I'm the woman, so I get to say what does or does not happen. After exchanging a few words, I walked over and sat next to him. He placed his arms around me and almost immediately, I knew I'd made a mistake. The smell of his cologne, the warmth of his body and the strength of his embrace made watching the movie almost impossible. Nevertheless, I kept staring at the television screen, trying to fight off those oh-so-familiar desires that were rising up in me. Suddenly, he kissed me on my forehead. That kiss was the invitation my flesh wanted, and after that, I fell into sexual immorality.

I knew I would have to share the news of my "fall" with my abstinence partner, and I knew that she would be screaming "I told you so" throughout the conversation. I felt guilty and I prayed over and over again for God to forgive me, but I felt like He was mad at me. My bragging days were over. I was officially in adultery. Suddenly, my relationship was more than just a relationship; it was a sexual relationship. For more than month, Clyde would come

by my house, and each time, I'd tell myself
that nothing was going to happen. Of
course, I kept failing miserably, and I kept
tearfully apologizing to God, all the while,
trying to figure out why I just couldn't stop
fornicating.

One day, I made up my mind to stop cold
turkey. I told Clyde that I was no longer
going to sleep with him and that he was no
longer welcome to my house. He lived out
of town, but he worked in a city near me.
He had to pass through my city on his way
home everyday. *By this time, Clyde was used
to me attempting to end the sexual part of our
relationship, so he didn't take me seriously.*
That night, he came to my house and
knocked on my door. The door had a small
window on it, so I looked out the window
and told him once again that he could not
stop by my house. I refused to let him in
because I knew that if I did, I'd be at God's
feet the next morning, pleading for His

forgiveness. While standing outside, he kept saying to me the same thing he'd said to me over the phone. *"You can't just sleep with a man and expect to just stop."* Because he wouldn't respect my wishes, I ended the relationship with him. Even after we broke up, Clyde continued to call me and reiterate his beliefs. He believed that since we'd already "crossed that line" that I didn't have the right to stop sleeping with him. Being knowledgeable of the Bible, he would often twist the scriptures and say that we were already "one", so our act was no longer a sin. Needless to say, I stopped accepting his phone calls altogether.

Why did I have trouble remaining pure? Because, like many single women, I didn't know what true purity was. I thought it was pretty much a sexual fast, and in that fast, a person would refuse to indulge in sex until an appointed time. My appointed time was marriage, but I could never seem to make it that far. But purity is so much more than just refraining from sexual activity; it is a heart condition that has been established on a series of beliefs, protected by proactive thinking and sealed by our love for God. I didn't have a pure heart because I didn't have enough Word in me to keep me from allowing myself to be tempted. I wasn't proactive; instead, I was reactive. In other words, I let each day fall into place as it would and I'd respond to whatever was going on at that moment.

Most people fail at abstinence because:
1. **They think they can outsmart their flesh.** The flesh is stronger than we give it credit for, and even the most astute Christians can fall under its lustful spell.
2. **They aren't proactive.** To be abstinent, you need to have a set of rules that you have committed to honoring. Additionally, you must

have a set of rules that you apply to whomever you end up courting. If that person refuses to follow the rules you've set, he is clearly not the God-sent spouse. Because of this, you should immediately end all communications with him.

3. **Bad associations ruin useful habits.** In my case, I was that bad association and I caused my friend to fall. After arguing with me about my choices, she became desensitized and ended up making the same mistakes I'd made. If you hang out with a fornicator, you'll slowly become desensitized to fornication.

4. **They are still married.** Anytime we have sex with someone, they become our spouses illegally. That's what fornication is. Fornication means to marry in the flesh without the vows, witnesses and the presence of God. When we are still married, our souls

will recognize us as married people.
A woman who is married has her
head uncovered by the man she's
joined herself to, but if that man
refuses to cover her, she will
subconsciously look for another
covering. What she doesn't realize is
that her soul is crying out for a
covering. A man who is illegally
married has uncovered a woman,
and because of this, he's responsible
for providing for her according to the
scriptures. His soul recognizes that
he is married, but his lack of
knowledge and understanding
causes him to reject his
responsibilities as a husband, all the
while, seeking the pleasures of
marriage. Because he refuses to
provide for the women he's lain with,
he uncovers himself (Christ is his
covering) and exposes himself to the
works of his own flesh.

5. **They haven't completely settled it in their hearts to be or remain pure.** Many people approach abstinence the same way they approach diets. It's just something they're trying on for the moment, but once the strength of their flesh challenges the weakness of their convictions, they return to what they know. Abstinence is a final decision; it does not have a trial period. When I fell, it was because I didn't understand abstinence and I hadn't completely settled it within my heart to remain pure. Instead, I was just trying on abstinence for size.

6. **They won't stop kissing.** So, what's the purpose of kissing? Many people who claim to be abstinent see absolutely nothing wrong with kissing their romantic interests. Kissing is foreplay! It's not an act to just show someone you love them;

kissing preheats the person and causes the body to prepare itself for penetration. It's actually harder to remain chaste when you're kissing someone than it is to walk away from them. Even kissing in public places should be forbidden by a Christian desiring to live a life pleasing to God. Let's be real here. Even if you become aroused in a public place, you can and likely will still fornicate. A sexually aroused person can be very creative, especially when lust clouds their thinking. The best route to take is not kissing at all. If the man you're seeing is your God-ordained spouse, he will have no problem waiting to kiss you for the first time at the altar.

7. **They keep trying to take their relationship to the next level.** A new relationship is almost always exciting, and it's normal to want to

show your love interest that you are serious about spending your life with him. But you've got to get it in your head that the person you are courting is possibly NOT the one God has for you. If you begin building with the wrong person, it'll be harder for you to let go of that relationship once it's revealed that it is not a relationship established by God. Courting is not about going from level to level; it's about getting to know one another while you wait to hear back from Heaven about one other. Sadly enough, many people in the church treat courting the same way the world treats dating, and because of this, many in the church end up with the same results as the world.

8. **They feel indebted to their love interests.** When the person you are courting (or dating) is not sold out

for Christ, they are going to use tactics, wiles, and devices to get what they want from you. So, that man you've been hanging out with may show up and give you a new bracelet. This may leave you feeling like you owe him something.

9. **They think they don't need God in their decision-making.** Here's the unwelcome truth: God has to be the head of every decision we make, but with most people who are anxious to be married, God falls behind their desires in their mental line-ups. So, their thoughts and plans are not in order; instead, they expect God to take a seat behind their lusts and desires. People make decisions and then, expect the Lord to sign off on their decisions — decisions He was not invited to take any part in. Because of this, they end up with the wrong people, being seduced,

tempted and led astray.

10. **They are in desperate need of deliverance.** Let's face it. Not everyone who thinks they are saved is really saved. The truth is — many people are serving the image of God that the world projects and they don't know the true and living God, JEHOVAH (YAHWEH). The world says fornication is expected. The world says fornication is a good thing. The world says that shacking is the new marriage. And because many who've involved themselves in the church have not yet separated themselves from the world, they are still engaging in worldly behaviors. Even believers need deliverance, but not from demonic possession; believers need deliverance from demonic oppression.

Of course, there are more reasons that

people find themselves failing at abstinence, but the aforementioned pointers are the most common reasons. One of the main reasons people fail is that they simply do not understand the purpose of abstinence. One of the things you'll come to realize about yourself is that anytime you don't understand a petition, you will question it, and in some cases, you will rebel against it. Not understanding a petition doesn't make the petition invalid. It only means that you need to dig a little deeper until you do understand the petition; that way, you won't waste your time questioning and challenging it. Think about your workplace. If your manager was to change the procedure of whatever it is that you are doing, and he was to make the new procedure mandatory, you wouldn't be happy because you are now being required to break a pattern. You may have mastered the old procedure, even though you weren't too crazy about it.

Nevertheless, you were used to that procedure and you were an expert at it, so it's only natural that you prefer the old over the new.

Even though the old procedure was outdated and costly, it worked, so you complain to management. The problem here is that you know that the old procedure was time-consuming, but you don't understand why the office made the changes. For you, the change makes no sense because the new machinery in itself was costly, plus, the new machines are some of the newest forms of technology. What if the manufacturers haven't completely worked out the bugs yet? Do you see how this pattern of thinking would cause you to be slack on your job and lower morale in the workplace? That's why it's necessary for a company to have meetings, especially when they are making changes. Employees often understand that changes

need to be made, but they do not
understand some of the changes that are
being made.

Companies hold meetings so that their
employees can get the understanding
they'll need to not only do their jobs but to
keep them encouraged as they do their
jobs. No company wants an office full of
disgruntled employees. The same goes for
abstinence. God wants us to understand
why He requires that we remain pure, but
He didn't exactly create a chapter in the
Bible and dedicate it to purity. Why is this?
Because the heart of fornication is
ignorance. If you read the Bible and you
ask God for understanding, you will better
understand the heart of God. So why is it
that God wants us to remain abstinent until
marriage?

1. **During sex, two people become one
   person, which means, they are
   united as one in God's eyes.** In other

words, the couple marries one another, although their union is ungodly and illegal. Marriage is a holy institution that mirrors our relationship with God, but when we enter fornication, we break into marriage illegally.

1 Corinthians 6:15 (NIV): "Do you not know that your bodies are members of Christ himself? Shall I then take the members of Christ and unite them with a prostitute? Never!"

2. **God wants us to be led by His Spirit and not by our flesh.** The flesh and the spirit are contrary to one another. The flesh wants to lead us, but the sin nature of the flesh causes it to rise up against God. This means that we should not be led by our carnal flesh since it will only lead us into sin and away from God.

Galatians 5:16-21 (ESV): "But I say, walk by the Spirit, and you will not

*gratify the desires of the flesh. For the
desires of the flesh are against the Spirit,
and the desires of the Spirit are against
the flesh, for these are opposed to each
other, to keep you from doing the things
you want to do. But if you are led by the
Spirit, you are not under the law. Now
the works of the flesh are evident: sexual
immorality, impurity, sensuality,
idolatry, sorcery, enmity, strife, jealousy,
fits of anger, rivalries, dissensions,
divisions, envy, drunkenness, orgies,
and things like these. I warn you, as I
warned you before, that those who do
such things will not inherit the kingdom
of God."*

3. **Sexual immorality defiles the land.**
   Because God gave man dominion
   over the earth and everything in it,
   He gave man the ability to release
   things (loose) into the earth and the
   ability to forbid things (bind) in the
   realm of the earth. When we sin

against Heaven, our sin defiles the earth and opens the door for demons. Of course, the enemy encourages us to sin so that we can open the door for him and everything that comes with him (sickness, disease, poverty, death, etc.).

2 Chronicles 7:14 (ESV): "If my people who are called by my name humble themselves, and pray and seek my face and turn from their wicked ways, then I will hear from heaven and will forgive their sin and heal their land."

4. **Unsevered soul ties destroy marriages.** God never designed us to be divorced. People change as the seasons in their lives change. Old thinking passes away, and our minds are always being renewed. Anytime we fornicate, we soul-tie ourselves to the people we've slept with. Because most of mankind does not recognize

this arrangement as an actual
marriage, most people get officially
married while still tied to others.
This is a sure-fire way to guarantee
that your "officiated" marriages
won't work; after all, the marriages
you've never made official (in the
eyes of man, at least) will affect you,
and they do affect you. They will
affect how you treat your husband,
whether you trust him or not, and
how you deal with adversity.
Because God did not create the soul
to be united to multiple people, any
and every breakup you've endured
has inflicted trauma to your soul. Of
course, when we give ourselves to
God and repent of our sins, He heals
and restores us. Nevertheless, our
minds still have to be changed; we
still have to get past the mental
trauma that we've had to endure.
After all, the memories don't fade

away. That's why you shouldn't be one in the flesh with anyone other than your husband.

1 Corinthians 15:33 (ESV): "Do not be deceived: "Bad company ruins good morals."

5. **Sex before marriage opens the door for adultery.** Most people think fornication simply means sex before marriage when this is not true. The Hebrew word for fornication is *porneia,* which means "harlotry." Harlotry is an inclusive word that means sexual immorality in any form, including sex before marriage, adultery, homosexuality, incest, whoredom, etc. Anytime you open the door to fornication, you open the door to every spirit that's associated with fornication, including the spirit of adultery.

Malachi 2:13-16 (NIV): "Another thing you do: You flood the Lord's altar with tears. You weep and wail because he no longer looks with favor on your offerings or accepts them with pleasure from your hands. You ask, "Why?" It is because the Lord is the witness between you and the wife of your youth. You have been unfaithful to her, though she is your partner, the wife of your marriage covenant. Has not the one God made you? You belong to him in body and spirit. And what does the one God seek? Godly offspring. So be on your guard, and do not be unfaithful to the wife of your youth. "The man who hates and divorces his wife," says the Lord, the God of Israel, "does violence to the one he should protect," says the Lord Almighty. So be on your guard, and do not be unfaithful."

6. **Purity drives away the Devil and thwarts his plans.** I always tell people that at any given moment, some woman is about to marry the

man who's going to eventually take her life. Had she submitted to God and just endured her seasons of singleness, as hard as they may have been, she would have likely been found by her God-appointed husband and she would have lived to testify. Anxiousness oftentimes leads people to early deaths, but purity scares the Devil away.

James 4:7 (ESV): "Submit yourselves therefore to God. Resist the devil, and he will flee from you."

7. **To strengthen the tie of the family unit.** To cleave means to unit with, become one with or to be tied to. When a person is soul-tied to several people, it is hard for that person to cleave to his or her spouse. Of course, this weakens the family unit and opens the door for the spirit of divorce.

Genesis 2:24 (KJV): "Therefore shall a

man leave his father and his mother, and shall cleave unto his wife: and they shall be one flesh.

8. **To ensure that men stick around to raise the children that they create.** Basically, God understands that men are creatures who will either embrace responsibility or shun it. A man who chooses sex before marriage is shunning responsibility; he is partaking in the pleasures of a wife without assuming the responsibility of having a wife. This behavior will follow him into fatherhood. When a man who's not ready for the responsibilities of being a husband is faced with the responsibilities of being a father, he will likely distance himself from his former lover and the child or children she bears for him. This leaves the child without a present father, and it oftentimes thrusts the

mother and the father into a contentious battle with one another. The mother feels cheated out of having a father for her child, whereas, the father feels as if he was dragged into a role that he was not ready for. Either way, the child finds himself or herself at the center of this battle, and it opens the child up for the spirits of rejection, unforgiveness, and low self-worth. At the same time, this sets the tone for the child's future relationships and the child is likely to follow in his or her mother's footprints.

Proverbs 22:6 (KJV): *"Train up a child in the way he should go: and when he is old, he will not depart from it."*

9. **To disallow the spirit of lust from being released.** People often say that once a person starts having sex, it's hard for that person to stop. Isn't it amazing that we can catch things in

the natural, but completely miss it in the spirit? When we are married and our "desire" has been awakened by our husbands, that desire is legal because it's under the authority of a covering. Everything is in order, so the desire isn't something that's been brought on by an unclean spirit. Nevertheless, any desire of the flesh that is not covered is called lust. Lust isn't just sexual; we can lust after a person's success, status, or material possessions. To lust after something means to have an ungodly desire for it. Whenever we participate in fornication, we give ourselves over to the spirit of lust because we begin to have ungodly desires toward the men we are sexually engaged with. For this reason, many women find themselves overwhelmed by desire to the point where they give in to other forms of sexual immorality including masturbation. Now, this isn't to say that a virgin cannot be bound by this spirit because they can and I've met a few who had somehow gotten that spirit in them. Fornication is one sure-fire way to let that spirit in and once you are bound by an ungodly desire, that desire will grow if you feed it. Eventually, it will consume you.

1 Corinthians 7:9 (ESV): "But if they cannot exercise self-control, they should marry. For it is better to marry than to burn with passion."

10. **To help us better understand our marriages to Him.** The church is referred to as the bride of Christ. Throughout the scriptures, God likens our relationship with Him to our relationships with our spouses. That's why the Bible tells husbands to love their wives as Christ loves the church (see Ephesians 5:25) and

wives are told to submit to their husbands as to the Lord (see Ephesians 5:22). When Israel began to worship other gods, God referred to their acts as "whoredom." We get a clearer illustration of our relationship with the Father through our relationship with our spouses. I remember crying out to the Lord many, many days when I was married to my second ex. I would go on emotional tirades about how he didn't love me, spend time with me, how he put others before me, how I was putting more into the marriage than I was getting out of it, etc. Each time, God would let me finish my tearful rant, and He would follow up my complaint with five very convicting words: "I know how you feel."

Isaiah 54:5 (ESV): "For your Maker is your husband, the LORD of hosts is his

> *name; and the Holy One of Israel is your Redeemer, the God of the whole earth he is called."*
>
> ***2 Corinthians 11:2 (NIV):*** *"I am jealous for you with a godly jealousy. I promised you to one husband, to Christ, so that I might present you as a pure virgin to him."*

Abstinence is a demonstration of our faith; it is our way of saying to God that we love Him, honor Him with our bodies and we trust Him. When we remain pure and wait for the husbands whom God has appointed to us, we show ourselves faithful to God, meaning, we display that we are ready to be wives. When we abstain from premarital sex, we are, in the same, making sacrifices to God because our choice to remain pure is going to drive away men who we are attracted to. It also makes us the objects of scolding, persecution and mockery. When we honor God with our minds, hearts, and bodies, God will reward us, even in the midst of those who once ridiculed and mocked us. At the same time, He will continually bless our marriages and use those marriages as demonstrations of His love and power.

Romans 12:1 (ESV): "I appeal to you therefore, brothers, by the mercies of God, to present your bodies as a living sacrifice, holy and acceptable to God, which is your spiritual worship."

Hebrews 11:6 (ESV): "And without faith it is impossible to please him, for whoever would draw near to God must believe that he exists and that he rewards those who seek him."

Psalms 23:5 (ESV): "You prepare a table before me in the presence of my enemies; you anoint my head with oil; my cup overflows."

Rebelling Against the Wait

Isaiah 30:9-14 (ESV): "For they are a rebellious people, lying children, children unwilling to hear the instruction of the Lord; who say to the seers, 'Do not see,' and to the prophets, 'Do not prophesy to us what is right; speak to us smooth things, prophesy illusions, leave the way, turn aside from the path, let us hear no more about the Holy One of Israel.' Therefore thus says the Holy One of Israel, 'Because you despise this word and trust in oppression and perverseness and rely on them, therefore this iniquity shall be to you like a breach in a high wall, bulging out, and about to collapse, whose breaking comes suddenly, in an instant; and its breaking is like that of a potter's vessel that is smashed so ruthlessly that among its fragments not a shard is found with which to take fire from the hearth, or to dip up water out of the cistern.'"

The fall of society is and was always preceded by rebellion. Rebellion, as defined by *Merriam-Webster's Dictionary* is:
1. opposition to one in authority or dominance.
2. open, armed, and usually unsuccessful defiance of or resistance to an established government.

Man's rebellion has always been against God. Since the fall of Adam, man has opposed the authority and dominion of God, and of course, their movement against Him has, was and will always be unsuccessful.

One of the principle reasons for rebellion is to attempt the overthrow of a government. God is all-powerful, and He has laid out laws to govern mankind, but many souls today don't want to abide by these laws, therefore, they rebel by disobeying God and erecting other gods in their lives. These false gods aren't always statues that people bow down to; oftentimes, they are false doctrines, relationships, and self.

God has given us a clear blueprint of what a romantic relationship should be. We are to seek Him first, and He will provide the relationships, the things and the lifestyles that we want. After that, we have to honor, love and respect God enough to remain pure until we are married. This can be difficult for a person who is anxious. The marital perks that most are anxious to receive include, but are not limited to:

Sex- If we're honest with ourselves, most of us can truly say that we look forward to having an all-access pass to our spouses. Nevertheless, this should be something that we look forward to and not something that we are struggling with. When people marry for the sole sake of having legal sex, they often end up in sexless marriages where they either lose their desire to have sex or they find themselves married to a spouse who doesn't care too much for sex.

Two-income household- In the United States and abroad, monthly living expenses can be pretty overwhelming at times. Most of us get by on our earnings and are able to live decent lives, but the prospect of having another person contributing makes the appeal of marriage almost irresistible.

Children- Truthfully, many people aren't waiting for marriage to have children, but for those who are, the idea of having children with the one man God has set aside is dreamy. As we get older, we tend to pay more attention to our biological clocks than we do to our Bibles, and for this reason, women who are approaching or have passed the thirty-year mark are oftentimes anxious to get married.

Having a life partner- Let's face it. We all

want to have a live-in best friend who
never leaves. We want to have that strong,
loving, and doting husband who laughs
with us, laughs at us, and cherishes our
very presence. We want to cuddle at night,
and we want someone to cook for (for
those who can cook) or someone to cook
for us (for those who can't cook). The idea
of having someone to spend our lives with,
go on vacations with, and just be happy
with is so appealing that romance books
are one of today's top book genres.

Unconditional love- We all want someone
to love our imperfect selves, regardless of
what we do or say. Of course, God gives us
this kind of love, but He Himself has
declared that it is not good for man to be
alone (see Genesis 2:18). We've had people
to give us brotherly love or the love of a
friend, but that love isn't always
accompanied by agape love, which, of
course, is unconditional godly love. Sure,
we are excited about being loved by our

Father, but we also want unconditional love from a human being. We want someone to spend our lives with— someone we can grow old with.

As man continues to pursue love, lust, and everything he thinks that marriage is, the stench of his rebellion continues to rise before Lord. The marriage bed has increasingly become more and more defiled as mankind tries to get the desires of his heart without having to be changed or having to wait on God. People today are anxious and the Bible tells us to be anxious for nothing (see Philippians 4:6). Today's rebellion has breached the once sacred bond of marriage. Since this foolish movement against God began, man has constantly tried to rewrite his own rules and laws, and man has tried unsuccessfully to overthrow the law of love that God has instituted for us to abide by.

Nowadays, sex is nothing but a casual act that takes place between two people who are driven to satisfy the lusts of their flesh in hopes that love will somehow spring forth from their sins. This tells us that many people today do not truly understand the law of sowing and reaping. We reap only what we sow; we cannot sow the seeds from an apple and expect an orange tree to grow in its place. We understand this when we speak of natural fruit, but why is it that most people don't understand this concept when it comes to spiritual things?

As mankind's relationship with God grows more and more distant, mankind's personal relationships lose their stable foundations and begin to crumble. Mankind is in rebellion and this rebellion has released a spirit of divorce into the earth.

I Samuel 15:23: "For rebellion is as the sin of witchcraft, and stubbornness is as iniquity and idolatry. Because you have rejected the word of the Lord, he has also rejected you from being king."

What exactly is witchcraft? Most people think of it as the powers of a mad woman with bad skin and a few missing teeth. *Merriam-Webster's Dictionary* defines witchcraft this way:

1. a: the use of sorcery or magic.
   b: communication with the Devil or with a familiar spirit.
2. an irresistible influence or fascination.

Isn't it funny how the world can define something, but not catch the realness of it all? Sorcery and magic are generic forms of power. There are two forms of power within the earth: the power of God and the powers of darkness. God's power is infinite and cannot be overruled because He is God and He is all powerful. The Devil uses the abilities that God has given him to move, speak, and shift things, and of course, he uses his abilities to do evil. This is the very definition of witchcraft.

The most eye-opening definition is *communication with the Devil or with the familiar.* The familiar, of course, is a familiar spirit. Therefore, when man rebels against God, he is under the influence of a familiar spirit. Familiar spirits work under the authority of Satan and are assigned to certain people. We are creatures of habit and Satan knows this. We tend to grow comfortable with familiar faces, familiar thinking patterns, familiar ways of life, familiar places and so on. No matter how wrong or deadly something is, if we've grown familiar with that thing, we feel no threat or harm can come from it. A good example would be a snake charmer who raises snakes for a living. Many grow comfortable with the snakes and often forget that the snakes can bite them. As a result, many are killed by the snakes they once charmed. The same goes for people who attempt to domesticate wild animals like lions, tigers, and bears.

Many have become too comfortable with the evils of this world because they have followed them for so long. People are fascinated with powers outside of God, not understanding that these powers are not only wicked and limited, but we have a greater power at work within us.
Luke 10:19 (ESV): "Behold, I have given you authority to tread on serpents and scorpions, and over all the power of the enemy, and nothing shall hurt you."

As the morals of mankind continues to sink, the lies that Satan sent out have become man's revised law. Divorce is widely accepted even within the once holy corridors of the church. Premarital sex is replacing marriages, promiscuity is widely accepted and same-sex unions are becoming the norm. We have been lied to and deceived by Hollywood's glamorization of fornication and every form of sexual immorality. The Bible refers to this as being bewitched, or better yet, being under the influence of demonic doctrines.

Galatians 3:1 (KJV): "O foolish Galatians, who hath bewitched you, that ye should not obey the truth, before whose eyes Jesus Christ hath been evidently set forth, crucified among you?"

Even the definition of love has been perverted to fit man's broken realities. This is why man's way never works. Instead, we keep getting entangled in relationships that have absolutely no substance or hope for a future. For this reason, the divorce rates in the United States alone continue to escalate and our nation continues to weaken. The nations around us shake their heads at us in dismay as we continue in our attempts to find some type of invention to pull us out of our dark pits. As God continually reaches down to rescue us, we ignore His all-powerful hand because we are so bewitched by beautiful lies that the truth has become unattractive to us. We are a nation of offended, broken, bitter, jealous, envious, and selfish people who want nothing more than to have a relationship with a man or a woman to replace our relationship with God. Each attempt proves to be unfruitful as no man has feet big enough to fit the shoes of the Lord. We have a God-sized hole in our hearts, but no amount of drugs, alcohol or sex can fill it. We need to return to Him so that we can be rescued from the dark lies that overshadow us.

People are crying out for love and jumping into one relationship after another, not understanding that God is love. He is the very definition and heart of love. He is the cure for our brokenness and our loneliness. This nation needs to be made whole again; this nation needs to return to its first love: YAHWEH!

We simply cannot have a successful relationship with a man or a woman without having a relationship with God. But this nation is "in love" with the lies that have been courting it. Again, this means that this nation has been bewitched. Sadly enough, many churches are falling into the same pits that the world has fallen into because many church leaders are following the world.

Matthew 15:4 (ESV): "Let them alone; they are blind guides. And if the blind lead the blind, both will fall into a pit."

Your relationship with a man or a woman will always mirror your relationship with the Lord. Even though this nation is broken, you can be restored, healed and set free from the bondage of ungodly thinking. You can have a successful relationship with a man or a woman when you have learned to have a successful relationship with the Lord. Even though we live in this world, we are not of this world. Their ways should not be our ways, and their beliefs should not be our beliefs. We don't have to go from one relationship to the next because God's order will keep us from disorder. Man's way reflects his attempt to be his own god and that's why he keeps failing. YAHWEH is God alone.

Rebellion is witchcraft and anytime you enter it, you have just entered into what I refer to as the witch's bedroom. The truth is that we must remain holy to see God. We cannot participate in fornication, regardless of how popular it is. We cannot choose which scriptures to follow and which ones to ignore. We will either serve God or we won't; the only alternative is to be lukewarm, and the Lord said that He would spit such a soul out of His mouth. This means that he will denounce them, or better yet, cast them out of His body. Sure, the world has their way of doing things, but we, as believers, cannot embrace the world's thinking or their ways. For us, such behavior is called rebellion and rebellion is so wicked in the eyes of God that He likens it to witchcraft.

John 14:6 (KJV): "Jesus saith unto him, I am the way, the truth, and the life: no man cometh unto the Father, but by me."

John 8:44 (KJV): "Ye are of your father the devil, and the lusts of your father ye will do. He was a murderer from the beginning, and abode not in the truth, because there is no truth in him. When he speaketh a lie, he speaketh of his own: for he is a liar, and the father of it."

1 Corinthians 14:33 (KJV): "For God is not the author of confusion, but of peace, as in all churches of the saints."

Let's revisit the story about my relationship with Clyde. I was in rebellion then because I knew that fornication was a sin. I chose to rebel because I didn't have enough Word in me to keep me and that made it easy for the enemy to deceive me. Because I chose to sin, I ended up losing the house and the car God had blessed me with. I'd gotten my house on pure faith! The owner had even paid the closing costs, which totaled up to more than $15,000. Howbeit, when I chose to rebel, I unknowingly chose to remove God as the authority in my life and I replaced Him with the one who comes to steal, kill, and destroy (Satan). He stole my house, my car and robbed me of most of what I had because I'd given him the legal rights to do so. My rebellion did not produce the blessings I wanted; instead, it robbed me of what I did have.

Don't allow the enemy to tempt you in rebellion. He'll promise to bless you and give you every desire of your heart, but once you give him the sin offering he needs to come in, he will rob you. He will not only rob you of the blessings of God, but worse than that, he will rob you of your relationship with God.

Maid for Him, Groomed for Her

Most people who desire to be married have already imagined what their lives are going to be like with their spouses. Many have begun preparing themselves to be spouses. On the outside, many are ready for marriage, but on the inside, they haven't touched the outskirts of understanding. This is because we aren't taught to build the inner-man or inner-woman; we are often taught to learn how to be better mates physically. This is one of the reasons the rate of divorce is on the rise.

To prepare yourself to be a bride or a groom, you must first learn to master being a son or daughter to the Most High God. You will never be a better spouse to a person than you are a child of God. This is the reason He told you to seek Him first.

God is setting you up to have a house of order because this is the only way your marriage will work. Satan thrives in disorder and disobedience, but he cannot function in order.

Another key element to getting ready is learning to respect the marriages of others. Pay attention to individuals who don't respect marriage. For example, men who often go after the wives of other men and women who often go after the husbands of other women rarely ever get married themselves. This is largely due to their way of thinking. No one wants to marry someone who does not respect the sanctity of marriage.

Respecting the marriages of others isn't just refusing to be a willing participant in adultery, but it is also having consideration for your married friends. For example, a woman should always know how to dress, speak, and behave around her friends' husbands. A friend who dresses provocatively or dances exotically around someone's husband is not a friend; she is a seductress. Additionally, covering for an adulterous friend, or allowing someone to commit adultery in your home is the same as being involved in adultery. Marriage is the unifying of two people in God, and therefore, should be treated with utmost respect.

Each woman of God is a maiden (virgin) until she lies down with a man. For this reason, many women who've never had marriage ceremonies don't realize they are still married. Nevertheless, once we are born again and we repent of our sins, we are given the blessed opportunities to be made whole again. God said that He would forgive us for our sins and remember them no more. We have to repent for those sins and finally commit to presenting our bodies and our minds as holy offerings unto the Lord.

Each man of God is a groom, but before he can wear his tuxedo and wait for his bride at the altar, he must first be groomed by God. God will bring him to the altar for salvation first, and then, back to the altar (repeatedly) for deliverance. He has to undergo the process of becoming a new creature in Christ Jesus before he's fit to be a husband. In other words, God begins to dress up his mind before He releases him to find his wife. That's why he's called a groom. God first grooms a man by saving him from eternal damnation, delivering him from the hands (strongholds) of the enemy, giving him a renewed mind and then disciplining him with the Word. A man has to consistently obey God until his mind is renewed and living righteously becomes his character.

Every woman in the Lord who desires to be married has a husband somewhere, but in order to be found by him, she must first become a maiden again. She must be washed of her past, and then, the Lord begins to clothe her in holiness and adorn her with wisdom, knowledge, and understanding. This process is designed to not only prepare her for marriage, but to prepare her for her assignment in the Lord. As the Lord dresses her up, He removes those filthy garments of sin and wrongful thinking, and He raises her up as a bride for Himself. She will undergo seasons of change that are designed to equip her for her next role as a wife. Once she has faithfully remained still in the Lord, she will then be ready to be found by her husband. Because she is hidden in the Lord, the enemy cannot reach her and that's why he will try to seduce her out of the Father's will. Going outside of the Father's will is similar to leaving her father's house and entering his enemy's house. In the enemy's house, she has given the enemy rights to do to her as he pleases. By staying in the Father's will, she stays hidden, and any woman who's hidden by God cannot be taken by the Devil. Satan can see her, but he cannot touch her.

Every man in the Lord who desires to be married has a wife somewhere. She's either being prepared for him, or she's ready to be found by him. Now, he must stay in the Father's will if he wants to find her. He must love the Lord with all his strength, mind, and soul until he is overtaken by love. This is the only way he'll learn to love himself and to love his wife as he loves himself. But before he starts his journey in the Lord, he must repent for all of the uncovered women he's left in his wake. When he truly repents, God will forgive his sins and remember them no more, and that's when he's free to find his wife. Of course, he must first be groomed to be a groom. He must be delivered from wrongful thinking, bad associations, and everything that's standing as a wall between him and the Lord.

Next, he must continue to seek the heart of the Lord to locate the will of God. In the will of God, he will find his identity. His identity is the same as his assignment. Because a wife is a help meet, her husband must already have his assignment in hand so that she can know what he needs help with. Once he receives and wholeheartedly accepts his assignment, he can then find his help meet, and he will find her hidden in the will of God.

Most people who seek marriage aren't seeking to be married for the right reasons. They are looking for ways to repair the cracks left in their souls by other human beings. Some people want financial partners. Some people want legal sex partners. Some people just want to say that they are married. Some people want to get married because their friends and loved ones are all married or getting married. People have many reasons for seeking the institution of marriage, but only a few know what marriage is and only a few are willing to accept the responsibilities of marriage.

God created many things in the realm of the earth to give us a better understanding of how marriage works. For example, on a job, you must work before you get paid. The same goes in marriage. You have to work at marriage before it yields a return to you, and you will only get out of marriage what you put into it. Unfortunately, many single souls think marriage is a one-way street where they'll be swept off their feet, flattered, taken care of, sexed, validated, and complimented day after day for the rest of their lives. Many of these souls imagine arguing with their spouses, and in their fantasies, each argument ends in a shower of love, sex, and repentance. Needless to say, such thinking is a shortcut to divorce court. This means that our minds have to be changed so that we can better understand the purpose of marriage. Marriage mirrors our relationship with God, therefore, in order for our marriages to work, we must be in right-standing with God.

Lastly, we must understand that we should not use our will to go out and choose our own spouses. Sure, God gave us free will, and we can exercise that will anytime we want to, but if we use it in the wrong way, we will reap from our choices. If we use our will in the right way, we pull down the blessings of God. We should always ask the Lord to introduce us to the spouses He wants us to have. Can we go out and choose on our own without being in sin? Of course, we can. But when we choose a life partner, we will always choose people in accordance with our way of thinking at that time, not understanding that our minds are going to constantly be transformed as we journey in the Lord. Because of this, most people who choose life partners for themselves end up growing apart from the people they've chosen. When God chooses our spouses for us, He won't send us people who match our right-now ways of thinking; He will send us spouses who match the renewed minds He has set aside for us.

A lot of people don't believe that God has designated that one special someone for them. After all, believing this means we have to change our entire view on relationships, marriage, and many of the things we've come to believe about life. Such thinking means that we have to tap

into a level of faith that most of us, quite
frankly, do not possess. At the same time,
this means that we cannot date every
beautiful soul who expresses interest in us.
Let's face it — we want our spouses and we
want them to come along quickly. We don't
know how long God is going to make us
wait, and this can be startling to someone
who's anxious to get married. At the same
time, if we don't believe that He has chosen
someone in particular for us, we then have
to question whether waiting would cost us
that once in a lifetime opportunity to get to
know someone who just may be a great fit
for us. Again, waiting for the appointed
one requires a whole new level of faith and
people nowadays don't want to build on
their faith. They simply want what they
want when they want it.

If we ask God to introduce us to the people
He has set aside for us, He will do so. If we
opt to choose our own spouses, we are not

in sin if the people we choose are single believers and we refrain from sexual immorality with them. Needless to say, however, if we choose our own spouses, we will choose people according to our fickle minds and marriages like these are very hard to maintain. When we trust God to choose for us, we are, in the same, saying that we trust God to head up those relationships as well. When we believe that the start of our marriages is God-ordained, we have no choice but to believe that those marriages cannot and will not be destroyed by the enemy.

Matthew 16:18: "And I say also unto thee, That thou art Peter, and upon this rock I will build my church; and the gates of hell shall not prevail against it."

Do We Really "Fall" in Love?

"O foolish Galatians, who hath bewitched you,
that ye should not obey the truth, before whose
eyes Jesus Christ hath been evidently set forth,
crucified among you" (Galatians 3:1)?

In America alone, there is a great
bewitching going on and many are falling
under its spell. People are so blinded by
lies and imaginations that they fall into the
deceptive traps of the enemy. What is this
great bewitching? It's called "falling in
love." In searching the scriptures, you will
find that this term has never once been
used, but instead, the Bible talks about love
and hate. There is no "falling in love" or
state of euphoria that brings us to such an
alluring, peaceful, and worry-free escape of
our personal realities other than a lie. A lie,
or better yet, self-manipulation is self-

bewitchment.

Romans 1:21-25: "Because, when they knew God, they glorified him not as God, neither were thankful; but became vain in their imaginations, and their foolish hearts were darkened. Professing themselves to be wise, they became fools, and changed the glory of the incorruptible God into an image made like to corruptible man, and to birds, and four-footed beasts, and creeping things. Therefore, God also gave them up to uncleanness through the lusts of their own hearts, to dishonor their own bodies between themselves: Who changed the truth of God into a lie, and worshiped and served the creature more than the Creator, who is blessed forever. Amen."

We all have an idea of what our perfect mates are like, and we often manipulate ourselves into believing that the person who is courting us is "the one" we've been waiting for all of our lives. Even when we see the signs that the guys in our sights are not the appointed ones for us, we also see a way to "fix" them. Maybe we can make them become our appointed ones or maybe we can fix them up so good that God will allow us to keep them. Instead of walking away, we pick up our tools and attempt to repair our potential spouses. Basically, we are carried away by our own desires.

There are many devices and schemes that the enemy has placed amongst us to aid us with this bewitching. They include today's music, television, and any other form of worldwide media. Let's say that you are in a relationship and your boyfriend calls you over to his place. He's turned on some slow, relaxing and romantic music. You're swept away with the words, the melodies, and the promises that fill the room from the artists' voice. You look up and your lover is staring you deep into your eyes and all of a sudden, that singer's promises seem to be your lover's promises. In that moment, you are in the state of "falling in love" or, in other words, being bewitched. If you allow this to happen to you, you will likely fall into the pit that the Bible calls sexual immorality. From there, you will begin to reap the consequences of your rebellion. For many, the consequences come in the form of being unwed mothers. Now, don't get me wrong children are a blessing and we all love them dearly. Howbeit, there aren't many women on the face of this earth who planned to raise their children without the fathers of those children being present. Of course, this is not to say that every woman who has children while married will remain married to their husbands; after all, statistics have proven otherwise. This is to say that sin has robbed us of many blessings. As for the women who do get married and end up divorced, the reality is— they likely married the wrong men or they married the right men in the wrong season. If we simply submit ourselves to God and stay in His will, we won't reap the results of the world. It's the unpopular truth, but it's the truth nonetheless.

I remember being sixteen years old and in a new relationship. I met "Travis" while at the mall one day. I was smitten with his face from the first day I saw him. As a matter of fact, I met him after my little sister had jokingly commented on how handsome he was, and then, proceeded to follow him (on his heels) throughout the mall. Laughing, he finally turned around, and we started talking.

Travis was young, but he was definitely an advanced charmer. Almost immediately, he began to say things to me that I'd never heard a guy say. He would play soft music in the background and if I tried to talk, he'd ask me to be quiet so that we could listen to the lyrics. I didn't realize what he was doing then; I thought he was genuinely falling in love with me, so I gave in. There would be long bouts of silence on the line, and then, he would break that silence with his soul-piercing words. His tone would be low and almost innocent as he said, "Tiffany, I think I'm in love with you." I didn't know how to react to this. I'd heard it once or twice before, but never in the way he said it. He sounded genuine; it was almost as if he believed his own lies. I would be silent, and then, I would tell him that I was in love with him as well, and then, we would return to silence.

During each conversation, my guard went down even more and Travis got more daring. Before long, he was talking about his desires to "make love" to me and to have a child with me. Now, anyone who knew me back then knew without a shadow of a doubt that I did not want to be a teenage mother. The idea of having some boy's baby and then having to face my mother was tormenting in itself. But for whatever reason, I found myself lowering my guard more and it wasn't long before I started agreeing with Travis. We made plans to consummate our relationship and try to have a child, but first, I needed to get around my mother. Thankfully, we never had a child together because it was difficult for us as teenagers to find a meeting place and then get someone to take us to that meeting place. Travis and I broke up after he had unknowingly asked the sister of a friend of mine for her phone number.

After Travis and I broke up, he stopped hiding his dark heart. We continued talking on the phone for a while, but he didn't feel the need to pretend to be the man he once advertised to me because I had made it clear that I wasn't going to reconcile with him. Travis began to tell me that he wanted to be like his father; he wanted to have children all around the world with women of just about every nationality. Years later, I came across Travis again, and he had followed through with trying to fulfill those dreams. He was only nineteen years old, and he already had anywhere between four to six children and he wanted more.

What Travis had done was very typical of a teenage boy, even though, as I stated earlier, he was pretty advanced at charming women. The reason for this was that he not only sounded genuine, but again, I think he believed his own lies. He had deceived himself into believing that he was genuinely in love with me and probably every woman who's ever given him the time of day. When a man is walking in this level of deception, it is very hard to discern him because he believes every word that he is saying. Nevertheless, when Travis realized that he and I were truly over, he stopped fooling himself and he introduced me to the person that he was. I can't lie and say that I didn't fall for Travis's deceptions again because I did when I was around nineteen years old. This, of course, was before I found out that he had several children, and he'd written off his old plans to spread his seed as nothing but the immature ramblings of a sixteen-year-old boy. Nevertheless, it didn't take me long to discover that Travis was still his old self and his plans for world domination were still very much active.

The point is— even though I was a young woman, I'd deceived myself because I believed everything Travis said. That's what bewitching is; it isn't necessarily being lied to. It means to believe the lies. There are a lot of liars in this world, but the Bible tells us to:

- Guard our hearts (see Proverbs 4:23)
- Cast down imaginations (see 2

Corinthians 3:5)
- Try the spirits (see 1 John 4:1)
- Put on the whole armor of God (see Ephesians 6:11)
- Be holy (see Leviticus 11:44)
- Present our bodies as living sacrifices (see Romans 12:1)
- Submit ourselves to God and resist the Devil (see James 4:7)

When we disobey God, we reap of the fruit of our rebellion. God's system is perfect; it cannot be overthrown or manipulated when it is executed consistently and with the right motives. No wrong man can stay in your life if you stay submitted to God; it's impossible for him to do so. No one can betray you without your permission. A lie cannot be forced upon an adult; it has to be believed to be received. This means that we deceive ourselves by believing others instead of believing the Word of God.

The people involved in an ungodly relationship both have individual ideas of what they want in a mate. The woman often believes that her new guy is this strong, protective, loving and doting man who will one day father her children and give her the life she wants. The man often believes that his new lady will be this soft, sensitive, motherly, and loving woman who will stay by his side despite his imperfections. The two then make love to the idea of what they want in one another, and if they do marry each other, they marry the idea of who they are and not the actual person standing at the altar. In most cases, such a couple will divorce one another's reality once they are no longer under the influence of the lies they've told themselves.

No one "falls" in love. We either love one another or we don't; that's the gist of it. Now, we do have emotional reactions to both love and lust and we often say of those feelings that we are "falling in love." This is not true. We are, in that hour, under the spell of a lie, and in the cases where we genuinely love a person, we are simply experiencing the newness of that love and we are responding to it. We lose ourselves in our imaginations and we like the way this feels. It makes us happy and it makes us want to give ourselves wholly to the people we have romantically linked ourselves to.

It is very dangerous to confuse emotions with love because emotions are unstable; they change with our beliefs, experiences, and as we mature. When someone says they are "in love" or have "fallen" in love, what that person is saying is quite frankly that they are under the influence of a new soul tie.

When I was a young woman, I had a friend

who'd "fallen in love" with a new guy in her life. She was young and inexperienced with relationships and her new guy was mesmerized by her. He wanted more than anything to be with her and she wanted to be with him. A couple of years after they met, she discovered that she was pregnant and this changed things between them. The allure of a new relationship had worn off and they were suddenly facing one of the greatest tests of love: responsibility. Responsibilities have a way of sobering us up and making us face the realities that we are in and not the fantasies that we've somehow gotten lost in.

After my friend discovered she was pregnant, her self-proclaimed fiance started having a change of heart. He suddenly realized that he was a young man and that there were a lot of things that he wasn't going to be able to do as a young father. That's when he started questioning whether or not she was worth the sacrifices he'd have to make to be her husband and to be a father to his child. He chose to abandon their relationship and pursue other women because he liked the newness of freshly started relationships. This is very common with young men and some older men alike. In other words, people actually like being under the influence of lies because they like how their minds and their bodies respond to new relationships. When we're in new relationships, we smile more, laugh more, and sing more. We rush home to talk with our new love interests, and we can't wait to spend time with them whenever possible. Howbeit, as time passes, we get to know the imperfect creature that the man whom we are courting is. This is when our emotions are tried and if love is not in us for that person (or vice versa), the relationship won't last. After all, there have been many of us who thought we loved a guy and as soon as we got to know him more, we discovered that not only did we not love him, but we didn't want to spend our lives with him. At the same time, men undergo this same process. It's unfair to think that every man who said he loved you before he left you had intentionally deceived you. This isn't always the case. Sometimes, men truly do think they love the women they are pursuing, but as time goes on, their feelings change. This signifies that what they felt wasn't love, even though at one point, they thought it was.

When Amnon set his eyes on his sister Tamar, he was in love with the idea of having Tamar. After raping her, he immediately began to hate her.
2 Samuel 1:13-15 (ESV): Now Absalom, David's son, had a beautiful sister, whose name was Tamar. And after a time Amnon, David's son loved her. And Amnon was so tormented that he made himself ill because

of his sister Tamar, for she was a virgin, and it seemed impossible to Amnon to do anything to her. But Amnon had a friend, whose name was Jonadab, the son of Shimeah, David's brother. And Jonadab was a very crafty man. And he said to him, "O son of the king, why are you so haggard morning after morning? Will you not tell me?" Amnon said to him, "I love Tamar, my brother Absalom's sister." Jonadab said to him, "Lie down on your bed and pretend to be ill. And when your father comes to see you, say to him, 'Let my sister Tamar come and give me bread to eat, and prepare the food in my sight, that I may see it and eat it from her hand.'" So Amnon lay down and pretended to be ill. And when the king came to see him, Amnon said to the king, "Please let my sister Tamar come and make a couple of cakes in my sight, that I may eat from her hand."
Then David sent home to Tamar, saying, "Go to your brother Amnon's house and

prepare food for him." So Tamar went to her brother Amnon's house, where he was lying down. And she took dough and kneaded it and made cakes in his sight and baked the cakes. And she took the pan and emptied it out before him, but he refused to eat. And Amnon said, "Send out everyone from me." So everyone went out from him. Then Amnon said to Tamar, "Bring the food into the chamber, that I may eat from your hand." And Tamar took the cakes she had made and brought them into the chamber to Amnon her brother. But when she brought them near him to eat, he took hold of her and said to her, "Come, lie with me, my sister." She answered him, "No, my brother, do not violate me, for such a thing is not done in Israel; do not do this outrageous thing. As for me, where could I carry my shame? And as for you, you would be as one of the outrageous fools in Israel. Now therefore, please speak to the king, for he will not withhold me from you." But he would not listen to her, and being stronger than she, he violated her and lay with her.

Then Amnon hated her with very great hatred, so that the hatred with which he hated her was greater than the love with which he had loved her. And Amnon said to her, "Get up! Go!"

Why did he hate her so much after he had her? It's simple: He was no longer bewitched with the idea of having her after he actually had her. The NIV translation says that Amnon was "in love" with his sister. I suspect that the author was trying to show that what Amnon had for Tamar wasn't actual love; it was more-so a desire to have her. What Amnon felt was not true love; it was the result of his ungodly thoughts of his sister. He likely believed that he genuinely loved her and wanted to spend his life with her and his friend Jonadab knew this. We can safely assume that Amnon was likely an inexperienced man who didn't know much about love or relationships, and Jonadab was his more experienced, ungodly buddy. He didn't advise Amnon to marry Tamar, even though in that time, a brother marrying his sister was not shunned when the siblings had different mothers. He advised Amnon to rape his sister because he knew that Tamar would never consent to have sex outside of marriage; she was an honorable and pure woman. Tamar was a virgin. Jonadab also knew that if Amnon were to marry his sister, he would likely discover that what he had for her was not true love. Being a devilish man himself, he told Amnon to rape Tamar, and when Amnon did, he immediately had a change of heart. As a matter of fact, before he followed through with the rape, Tamar had attempted to reason with him. He had plenty of time to consider what she was saying and maybe even ask David for her hand in marriage, but that wasn't the nature of his desire towards her. He probably had a bunch of sexual fantasies and confused his desires for love. This is very common with young, inexperienced adults.

Remember the story I told earlier about an ex of mine by the name of Ivan. Ivan had reached out to me twenty years later in an attempt to reconnect romantically with me. I rejected him for several reasons, but the main ones were:

- He was still married; his divorce had not been finalized.

- He was not in Christ Jesus.

- He suggested that we would engage in premarital sex when he told me that I would likely be pregnant by him before we got married.

Now, I want to be honest here; I did like

Ivan. We talked for a total of three days, and even though this isn't a long time, we had spent the better part of those three days catching up. Ivan knew what he wanted. He wanted to get married (or better yet, remarried) and he wanted a faithful, doting wife. He and his wife were divorcing because she had left him to be with another man and, it goes without saying that he wanted someone to replace her. This is normal for a person who is going through a divorce and wanting to relieve themselves of the pain associated with a divorce.

In those three days, I discovered that Ivan and I (in the flesh) would have been great together, but Ivan and I would have been spiritual enemies, which, of course, would have eventually carried over into our flesh. (When I say "in the flesh", I'm not talking about sexually; I'm talking about common interests.) Ivan was the perfect candidate for the old Tiffany. Anytime I share that story with others, I tell them that if I did not stop communicating with Ivan, we would have likely been married within three to six months. Ivan wanted to get remarried, and I wanted to get remarried. We both wanted faithful spouses; we had that much in common.

Because of our common interests, I found myself getting excited every time Ivan called me. Even though I knew that he wasn't the God-sent one, I kept trying to entertain the idea that he was. In other words, I started intentionally attempting to deceive myself because I liked how it felt to be caught up in all the excitement associated with a new and promising relationship. So, when Ivan called me, my heart would flutter and I would smile, but again, the Lord rebuked me and I had to cut all ties with Ivan. I didn't realize what I was doing until the Lord addressed me. He told me that I was opening myself up for an ungodly soul tie. I was doing like so many believing women do. I was telling Ivan about my convictions and hoping that by him agreeing to honor my wishes to remain pure and to serve God that somehow, my wait would be over. I had to open myself up to the truth: Ivan was not my God-appointed husband and by entertaining him, I was entertaining the spirit of adultery. It didn't matter that Ivan and his wife had already signed the divorce papers; in God's eyes, they were married and he was off limits. At the same time, in God's eyes, I am married to Him, and therefore, off limits to any man who is not in Christ Jesus. This is to demonstrate how easy it is for us, as women, to pretty much deceive ourselves. In order for me to walk away from Ivan, I had to hear from Heaven and tell myself the not-so-friendly truth: Ivan and I would have had a wonderful honeymoon, but a disaster of a marriage.

We don't "fall" in love; we fall into the snares of lust and ignorance. We fall because we're impatient, and while we are waiting for God to send our appointed spouses to us, we are being presented with opportunities to have everything we think we want in other men. We fall when we choose the lies over the truth. When the Bible speaks of the word "fall," it is often speaking of mankind falling into sin (rebellion) or falling because of sin (judgment). Yet, the Bible speaks of God as love and this tells us that love is not a fall; it's our decision to stand up and follow our God, instead of falling into the traps of the enemy. Love is not an emotion; it is a spirit and that's why the Bible says that love never fails. Feelings change, people change, but love always remains the same. We don't "fall" in love; we fall into temptation, but love lifts us up and covers us, even when we're undeserving of it.

The One Who Got Away

After many years, an old friend of mine
found me and contacted me. We hadn't
talked in years, and I was somewhat
surprised to hear from her. At the same
time, I knew why she wanted to reconnect
with me. It was because of an ex-boyfriend
of hers who she was still in love with— an
ex-boyfriend who I happen to be related to
(through marriage). Nevertheless, I didn't
shun the conversation because I knew she
was a woman of God, and I knew that she
was just having one of those moments
where she was considering what could
have been.

Over the years, I have watched this man
(her ex) go through women and leave them
just because they'd dare to disagree with
him. He is spoiled, prideful, and pompous,

and I have always said that I pitied the woman who married him. He didn't desire to have a wife to make her happy; his desire was to have a human slave whose mind he could rearrange for his own personal pleasure.

After this old friend contacted me, I went back and forth in my head as to whether or not I should directly tell her to go somewhere and glorify God for not letting that relationship work. I didn't want to talk about him negatively, but at the same time, I knew that she was a really good girl who deserved better. I decided to just let the Lord lead me in my conversation because I didn't want to dabble with gossip. I decided to not say anything about him, and if she brought his name up to me, I would simply tell her to thank God because He is and was protecting her. Eventually, she did bring him up, and I could tell that she was still angry with her mother for ruining her relationship with the man she believed to be the love of her life. That was it. I decided to tell her outright that God had been truly protecting her from the guy, but of course, I exercised wisdom to ensure that I did not gossip about him. This was hard for me because there is a fine line between telling a story and gossiping, and I didn't want to cross it, nevertheless, I knew she needed to hear about how he'd treated a few other women. That way, she could stop wondering about him and move on. I shared a couple of stories with her and told her how he'd treated a few women he had been pursuing. She was shocked and it was as if I could see the shackles falling off her. Her shock turned to relief, and before long, she was thanking God that she didn't marry the guy.

Over the years, I have seen many situations like this. When I was unsaved, I wouldn't hold back; I would be honest with the women and tell them that they needed to be thankful that the relationship didn't work out. Nowadays, I'm still honest, but I try to exercise tact and wisdom in my dealings. I know that when a relationship ends and there are a lot of unanswered questions, some people feel they need closure to move on, especially if those relationships ended because of the interference of another person. Closure starts on the inside of each individual. Basically, closure is nothing but (1) coming to the realization that the relationship is over, and (2) understanding why the relationship was not a good idea.

When we verbally request closure from the person we were in the relationship with, it's not because we actually want closure. In most cases, we want to talk about the issue and smooth out all of the problems in an attempt to jump-start the relationship. This usually happens when a woman has not prepared her heart for the breakup and is looking for any signs of life in that relationship. For example, when I was married the first time and my ex was packing his bags, I was frantic and I kept following him while he packed. I repeatedly asked him for closure, but closure wasn't what I truly wanted. Even though I knew our marriage was not going to work and I knew that he was leaving me for someone else, I wasn't ready to end the relationship at that time because it was all sudden. My pleas for closure were nothing more than my attempts to delay the inevitable. Did I plan to stay with him for the long haul? No. I had given up on the idea of us spending our lives together because of his adulterous affairs and his temper. I knew our marriage was doomed, but like many broken women, I wanted to slowly transition out of that marriage. I was afraid of suddenly being single, so I tried to stop him from leaving by asking for closure. Thankfully, he did not honor my request, and God showed me that I could go on without him. I decided to completely release him in every way so that I could move on with my life, so I asked the Lord to put forgiveness in me towards him, and He did.

The problem with a lot of us is that we don't ask God to close those doors between us and our past lovers because we are unsure of our futures. Quite frankly, we are afraid of futures that we haven't planned for ourselves, and God knows this. I chose to release my ex, not just because of his ways, but I chose to release him because I sincerely wanted to be loved. I wanted to be married to a faithful man who not only loved me, but loved the Lord even more. I didn't lie to myself. I told myself the hard truth; my ex wasn't good for me, and I needed to let him go.

In America, we have coined the term, "the one who got away." This implies that a good and potentially lasting relationship ended suddenly because of human interference or a sudden move. The truth is that there are many believing women who have at least one man that they feel they were robbed of. Maybe the guy's mother did not approve of them or maybe he was sent away to boarding school. Nonetheless, when a woman believes that one of her exes was unfairly snatched from her grip, she will not release him in her heart. She may give up on the idea of ever being with him, but she won't throw away the idea entirely. She will entertain it in the back of her mind, not understanding that her refusal to fully release her ex has stopped her from meeting her God-assigned husband and has ruined many of her past relationships. What's amazing is that we can all say without a shadow of a doubt that the Bible is the Word of God and that

God has supernaturally protected its contents. He has not allowed it to be tainted by wicked men (or women) and He has ensured that the infallible Word of God make its way into our homes and eventually into our hearts. Nevertheless, the average woman does not believe that God has supernaturally protected her from the wrong men by driving away every man who attempted to make her his own. Believe it or not, God has kept us, even when we didn't want to be kept. What this means is— the one who got away was more than likely not our God-appointed husbands.

Thankfully, for me, I can sincerely say that there is no man in my past that I see as someone who's gotten away, or better yet, could have possibly been the right man in the wrong season. The guys from my past were nothing but choices I made when I was in the darkness of sin and blinded by

my own selfish desires. And they can say
the same for me. The point is— you need to
release your past and everyone in it if you
are entertaining the idea that some man
you've met or have been romantically
linked to is "the one who got away." God is
all-knowing, all-powerful, and perfect in all
His ways. He has the ability to
supernaturally connect you with the one
He has assigned you to and He will do this
in the season that He has arranged for you
to get married.

People often entertain the idea that one of
their exes was their "soulmate" when
neither they nor their ex can bear the full
blame for the ending of those relationships.
At the same time, people do this when they
are fully at fault and haven't met someone
who has loved (or tolerated) them in the
manner in which one of their exes did. For
example, I have heard a few guys express
interest in rekindling their relationships

with some of their exes, but this desire wasn't because they love the women. It was because they had cheated on those women and the women had stuck with them despite all they had put them through. Eventually, the guys abandoned their relationships or marriages to pursue other women, but those women weren't as tolerable as their exes. Instead, their mistress-turned-lovers cheated on them or left them for other men. In some cases, they were still in relationships with the women they had left their previous relationships for, but again, their current lovers weren't as patient, loving or tolerable as their exes. Their desires to rekindle their relationships with their exes were completely selfish. They wanted to reconcile with their exes because they had come to realize that they weren't one-women men. They knew that they would have extramarital affairs and they wanted a woman who would stick with them throughout it. Understand this:

Not every cheater wants to be a bigamist.
Some cheaters want wives, children, homes
and everything we identify as the
American dream, but they also want one or
more mistresses. Oftentimes, this is because
they need deliverance and renewed minds
(of course), but most of the guys I'm
referring to don't want to be changed. They
love their sins and they love themselves,
but they don't know how to love anyone
else. That's why they can never seem to get
over any woman who puts up with their
adulterous ways. Those guys would
happily refer to their tolerable exes as their
"soulmates." This is why we can't allow
ourselves to be flattered every time one of
our exes expresses interest in rekindling a
relationship with us. Sometimes, a man's
desire to restart a relationship with a
woman he has wronged is an indirect
insult, where he pretty much believes that
she will stick with him despite his
wrongdoings. He's not saying that she was

the best woman he's ever had; he's not even saying that she's the woman he wants to spend his life with. All too often, what a man is saying is that the woman he's pursuing either deserves what he plans to take her through or she's strong enough to endure it without leaving him. Believe it or not, many (broken) men think this way.

Who's the one that got away in your life and are you still soul-tied to him? Are there any men out there who you would reconcile with if you were given the chance? These are very important questions for you to ask yourself to ensure that you're not being held back or hindered by an unsevered soul tie. Again, there is no one person who "got away" from you. If it was meant to be, and you are in the will of God, it will happen in due season. Remember, God is all-knowing, meaning, He will not assign us to marry people who He knows we will never get around to marrying.

Rejection or Protection

Your exes were weapons formed against you, but the question is— did they prosper? At the same time, let's be fair. You may have been a weapon formed against one or more of your exes as well. Truthfully, when we start to take accountability for our own wrongs, it makes it easier for us to forgive people and make better decisions. We get into relationships not headed up by God when we have not completely submitted ourselves to God.

We tend to underestimate the kingdom of darkness by placing much of the blame for our pain, betrayals, and unforgiveness on people. The truth of the matter is— we are given the opportunity to choose between good and evil; God does not force us to choose Him. When we choose sin over righteousness, we reap the consequences of our sins, and those consequences can be painful. Sometimes, the pain is almost unbearable. It puts me in the mind of what my mother used to say to me whenever she was disciplining me. In the midst of getting a whooping, I'd cry out that the belt was hurting me, and she'd respond, "It's not supposed to feel good."

The enemy is strategic; we've got to understand this. He knows that once our hearts have been broken, we will go to extra lengths to ensure that our hearts aren't broken again. Now, here's the problem. In our attempts to protect ourselves from being hurt, we end up hurting others, all the while, opening ourselves up to be hurt even more. In other words, our strategies don't work. They only backfire and they serve to get us further away from the will of God. Again, the enemy is strategic. He presents false wisdom to us and tells us how to "play the game" of life and in relationships. This is a game that we end up losing repeatedly, and while we're off somewhere trying to master relationships and people, the enemy is busy attacking our hearts. Every time we fail, our hearts are broken all the more. That's why following the Word of God is the only way to protect ourselves.

As you've already read in this book, I was married twice. Both times, I did it outside the will of God. The first time, I married when I was a babe in Christ and the second time, I married when I was still an immature believer. This is to say that I chose men for myself who represented where I was and not where I was going. Because of this, those relationships were not built on the right foundations, so they did not survive the tests of time. One thing I've discovered is— anytime we build relationships and lives for ourselves, those relationships and lives will be tested. If God is not in them, they will not survive the tests.

1 Corinthians 3:10-15 (ESV): "According to the grace of God given to me, like a skilled master builder I laid a foundation, and someone else is building upon it. Let each one take care how he builds upon it. For no one can lay a foundation other than that which is laid, which is Jesus Christ. Now if anyone builds on the foundation with gold, silver, precious stones, wood, hay, straw — each one's work will become manifest, for the Day will disclose it, because it will be revealed by fire, and the fire will test what sort of work each one has done. If the work that anyone has built on the foundation survives, he will receive a reward. If anyone's work is burned up, he will suffer loss, though he himself will be saved, but only as through fire."

Those marriages did not survive because they were not built on the solid foundation which is the Lord. They were established on flesh, for flesh. If I was bitter about the ending of those marriages, it would only mean that I didn't have the understanding I needed to move forward. I understand why they didn't work and I hold myself accountable for the ending of those marriages. How so? It's simple. I should not have disobeyed God. I can't go into sin, come out with sinners, and then complain when they sin against me. In other words, I reaped what I sowed and because I understand this, I was able to forgive my exes and move forward. Nowadays, I've chosen to live life God's way. I refuse to entertain unequally yoked relationships, and I've chosen the purity path.

I can't tell you how many wounded women I've come across on my path, and the sad part is— many of them are in ministry.

They have established ministries on the foundation of their pain, and they aren't looking to be set free. Instead, they like the victim label and that's why they seek out other hurting women so they can have someone to complain with. If you join their ministries and you're a hurting woman, the minister will take you under her wings, and then, she'll proceed to speak word curses over whomever you say has hurt you. This is a witchcraft ministry and it was established by Satan to catch hurting women who are looking to avenge their broken hearts. I've seen ministries like this countless times and the sad part is— they are filled with angry, vengeful and vindictive women. Now, this isn't to say that every ministry established by a woman for hurting women is a witchcraft ministry, but you need to be very watchful and definitely test the spirit of the leader at any and every church you find yourself in. A good way to tell if a ministry is established by an unforgiving soul is to (1) listen to her; after all, out of the abundance of the heart, the mouth speaks, and (2) testify. One thing I've discovered is anytime I testify about what I've gone through, if I'm in the presence of an unforgiving woman, she will attempt to speak evil over my exes. Of course, she will try to disguise her evil words as prophecies or words of knowledge, but her anger towards them is not a reflection of her love for me. It's a reaction of her unforgiving heart. The heart of love makes you want to intercede for people, but a heart of hatred makes you want to curse them.

Matthew 7:16 (ESV): "You will recognize them by their fruits. Are grapes gathered from thornbushes, or figs from thistles?"

1 John 4:1 (ESV): "Beloved, do not believe every spirit, but test the spirits to see whether they are from God, for many false prophets have gone out into the world."

Understand this— you chose the guys who've rejected you. You accepted them into your life because of where you were spiritually and what you thought they could bring to your life. The relationships were not built on the foundation of faith, even if they were established in the church. Faith-based relationships are established on the Word and headed up by the Word. The substance of those relationships is holiness, purity, obedience to God, and purpose. Your intentions for getting with one another have to be centered around the idea of marriage and then you have to ensure that you don't give your guy husband-benefits when he is not yet your husband. Your relationship has a starting point and it has to have a focal point, meaning, you should both have a mutual understanding of where you're trying to get to. If marriage isn't the focal point, you shouldn't be in that relationship. If the guy is unsure as to where he wants that relationship to go, you shouldn't be in that relationship. The great thing about being intentional is that it scares away men who want the pleasures of having a wife but shun the responsibilities of being husbands.

As of right now, I'm not courting anyone, but I have met three guys over the two years that I've been single. I can't really say that one of them was an actual relationship pursuit because it was a blind date that I agreed to go on because a friend was pressuring me to do so, but I knew before I met the guy that he wasn't the one. Thankfully, he was nice about it and we parted ways after we met. He was a Christian man who loved the Lord, but I knew he wasn't the one; I didn't need a prophecy to get that revelation.

The second guy approached me in a laundromat and insisted that I allow him to carry my laundry. I was reluctant, but he wouldn't take no for an answer. While in the parking lot, he asked for my phone number, and I made the mistake of giving him my number before I asked him about his relationship with the Lord.

Nevertheless, after I gave him my number, I suddenly remembered to ask him and I found out that he believed in God, but was not an active believer. He was a secular man, so I told him while in the parking lot that he was not my husband. Of course, he didn't agree, and he ended up calling me a few times before I asked him to stop calling. Of course, the last guy was Ivan (the ex) and after three days of talking with him, I ended all communications with him. Why am I telling you this? I'm sharing this with you because you have to understand that God has given us a template to go by and that template is Jesus Christ. If a man is not in the Lord, he is not the one God has appointed for your life— end of story. The old Tiffany would have thought that she could change any one of the last two guys, but the woman that I am today knows better. Those relationships would have ended with a rejection far worse than me telling them that it was best if they didn't call me anymore. A woman telling a man that he is not the one is a small bruise to his ego, but letting down a man who has invested in you can be devastating and that's why I don't lead men on. If I know that the guy who's pursuing me isn't the one, I tell him. I don't spend a week or a month entertaining him, and hoping that God will change His mind about the guy.

Many of us have been hurt or rejected at some point, and it's pretty overwhelming when we've invested our time and bodies into those relationships. That's why God wants us to remain pure and that's why He told us to not yoke ourselves with unbelievers. In other words, God warned us, but did we heed the warning? Most of us did not, and we reaped of our choices. That's why it's silly for a woman to walk around mad at her exes. What I've come to understand is that sometimes, it wasn't the guys who betrayed and walked away from us. I genuinely believe that God drove many of those guys away because they had rejected Him. This is especially true for the women who are entering seasons where they are to be used by God in ministry.

Anytime we choose men who have rejected our God, we are choosing to be rejected by those men should we continue to follow the Lord. Darkness and light cannot coexist, and try as we may, we don't have the power to make a crooked man straight. God does not infringe upon a man's will and neither can we. This means that rejection is oftentimes God's way of protecting us. As I mentioned earlier, there is a woman somewhere exchanging vows with the man who will someday take her life. This is what God is protecting us from! When we cry and complain about relationships that didn't last, it's because we don't know what God knows. He knows where He's called us to be and what He's equipped us with. He also knows what we can and cannot bear, and the truth is— some men are unbearable to some women. For example, when I testify about much of what I'd gone through in my marriages (adultery, stalked by mistresses, physical abuse, verbal abuse, witchcraft, etc.), it is not uncommon for me to hear women say that they don't know how I survived it all. It is not uncommon for me to hear women say that they would have killed or maimed my husbands had they been married to them. This means that the ability to withstand what I'd gone through was graced to me by God, but not every woman can receive this amount of grace. The reason for this is that not every woman is willing to extend the kind of grace that I extended in those marriages. You have to understand that you need to give grace to receive more grace. I was tolerant, forgiving, and hopeful in both marriages, and I gave up on those marriages once the guys had given up on me. In other words, I let the unbelievers choose to leave in both cases. When they left, they only confirmed the Word of God. This helped to open my eyes and I understood that there was and is no shortcut around God's way.

2 Corinthians 6:14 (ESV): "Do not be unequally yoked with unbelievers. For what partnership has righteousness with lawlessness? Or what fellowship has light with darkness?"

Mark 3:25 (ESV): "And if a house is divided against itself, that house will not be able to stand."

Anytime a woman marries an unbeliever, what happens is— the woman brings her

God into the marriage and the husband brings his gods into the marriage. In most cases, the wife will try to lead her husband to Christ and the husband will try to get his wife to accept him as he is. He will then proceed to introduce her to his gods. He's not the one to blame for the failing of that relationship entirely. It is the responsibility of the believer to follow the Word of God. We cannot expect the unbeliever to follow the Word when he is not yet saved.

But what if you were rejected by a believing man? Remember, I mentioned earlier that a friend of mine tried to introduce me to a believing man, and I agreed to have a blind date with him. I knew he wasn't the one from the moment we talked on the phone, but by then, I had already agreed to meet with the guy at a local restaurant. He was a true believer; it was clear that he loved the Lord, so we behaved as sisters and brothers in the Lord.

I think we mutually knew that we weren't for one another, so there were no hard feelings or harsh words. We just parted ways and that was the end of it. Now, every relationship between believers won't end like this, especially since the guy and I didn't have a relationship. But what if you did have a relationship with a man and he suddenly rejected you? You have to understand that his rejection is more than likely the result of God speaking to him and saying that you are not the one or he may have come to this realization on his own. Sometimes, God doesn't have to tell us that another person isn't for us. We know this by how different they are from us and how different their goals and views are from our own.

Sometimes, believing men reject believing women because:

1. **The man himself is not completely right with God.** The closer you are to

God, the more likely you are to run off double-minded Christians. This includes the ones who stand behind pulpits and wear religious titles. My closest (single) friends are abstinent and they can tell you stories of believing men (including ministers) who stopped calling them the minute they revealed that they were abstinent. Their choice to follow God drove away the wrong men and this is a good thing; it's not bad at all! Could you imagine being married to a fornicating minister who couldn't keep his hands off the sheep he's supposed to be covering?

2. **The woman is not in right-standing with God.** Let's face it— not every woman who cries Lord is actually saved and not every lady who practices abstinence is actually pure. When a man is truly in submission to God, He will warn the guy about any

woman he chooses to court. After all, that's the purpose of courtship. It isn't just for two people who like each other to hang out until the guy proposes and they get married. The main purpose of a courtship is to hear back from God regarding the person you plan to court.

3. **God has spoken to the man and revealed that the woman he's pursuing is not his wife.** Just because two people love the Lord doesn't mean they'll be good together. I can use myself as an example— I've traveled to many countries, I have done a lot of things in my life and I want to do more. I want to visit many more countries, learn a language or two, possibly live abroad someday, have a couple of children, write thousands of books, birth a few of my invention ideas, buy properties and sell them, etc. In

other words, I want an active life
because I have an active mind.
Besides Ivan not being a believer, he
was also an inactive man. He had
never visited another country, nor
did he have any interest in doing so.
He would have wanted me in the
house, cooking, cleaning and having
babies. I would have been unhappy
with him because I'm an
adventurous woman. I don't mind
cooking; I definitely keep a clean
house, and I do want children, but I
also want to get out and see the
world. I want my children to learn a
few languages, write books while in
their youth, etc. So, a believing man
who's scary or inactive would not be
a great match for me. Now, this isn't
to say that God wouldn't send a guy
like that to me (and then laugh while
I pleaded with Him to change the
dude), but it is to say that I am

designed the way that I am designed because I am my husband's help meet. I'm similar to my husband, even though I have not yet formally met the guy. If another believing man was to pursue me, he'd likely run away because I wouldn't fit into his vision of what a wife is or what a wife does— especially if he was one of those leaders who didn't believe women should teach.

4. **He just didn't like the woman enough to pursue her any further.** I think this is the more common reason that some men end their pursuits. This isn't wrong for the guy to do because sometimes, we pursue people when we don't know much about them. As their character, habits and ways are revealed to us, we do changes our minds. After all, that's one of the reasons we court before marrying. We are trying to get to

know the other person, and again,
some women can't bear some men
and they find this out in the
courtship. The same goes for men.
Some guys discover that they cannot
bear or tolerate the women they are
courting, so they end the courtship.

It doesn't matter why the guy ends the
relationship, the most important thing is
that we remain in the will of God and we
do not allow ourselves to become bitter.
God protects us and we know this, but we
have to start following the Word of God
and guarding our hearts. We do this by not
assuming that every cute man who says,
"Praise the Lord" is our God-appointed
husband. We test the spirits, remain
prayerful, practice purity, and stay in the
will of God so that if the guy is not from
God, he will reject us. Truthfully, we
should want to be rejected by the wrong
men; I really don't understand why it's

even an issue. I would have preferred that my exes rejected me from the start than to have ended up divorced twice, but that is my story now. I choose to testify to ensure that other women don't end up falling into the pits I've fallen into. I don't regret either of those marriages. I sincerely believe that they both woke me up and helped me to find my place in Christ, but at the same time, I would have preferred to have been a woman who believed God without having to experience what I've experienced than to have been the stiff-necked, stubborn soul that I was. Rejection is God's protection in most cases, and yes, this includes situations where there was human interference.

Trying to Save The Unsaved

Imagine yourself reaching out your hand to a person who has gone over the cliff of a mountain. He is holding onto a sharp rock and screaming for your help. You are doing what you can do for him by extending your hand to him. All he has to do is grab your hand and try to help you pull him up. However, he simply keeps both hands on the rocks while screaming and begging for your help. On the left side of the mountain, someone else has gone over the edge, and he too is holding onto a sharp rock, but he is trying to pull himself up. He has asked for your help a few times, and you've extended your hand to him, but he decided that he could pull himself up and didn't need your help. He did, however, want you to stand within his view just in case he found himself slipping again. Finally, on the back of the mountain, someone else has gone over the edge and suddenly screams out for your help. You race over to see if you can save the person and you ask for his hand. He puts his hand in your hand and begins to pull himself up to safety. You ask the newly rescued soul to go to the right side of the mountain to help the guy who refuses to take his hands off the rock. You tell him to share how he was just rescued to encourage him to reach up and grab your hand. You then go to the left side of the rock, because even though the guy appears to need the least help, he actually needs the most help because he is spending his strength trying to pull himself up.

Now, imagine the Savior is Jesus Christ, and the three fallen people are you, your God-chosen future spouse, and the unsaved mate you chose for yourself. Which one of these fallen souls would you consider yourself to be? Would you be the

one who has grabbed onto God's
unchanging hand, the one who is too
fearful to let go of what they know, or
would you be the soul who insisted on
doing it all for yourself? Let's say that you
are the one who was rescued, and you were
told to go and help the one who was afraid
to reach out, but you chose to go and try to
help the one who wanted to do it on his
own because you were smitten by his
determination and his good looks. You
reach down to pull this character up, but
instead, he pulls you down to an imminent
death alongside him because he'd spent all
his energy trying to do it by himself. You
thought that because this character had
asked for God's help initially, he was
almost saved, but he just needed a helping
hand. Instead, you found yourself falling
with him. During this fall, the reality sets
in— a person is either saved or they are not;
there is no such thing as almost saved.

How many people do this? You say that you have given yourself to the Lord and you have been saved, but you keep looking for a spouse amongst the fallen. You have to understand that your mate is not found in the unsaved, but your mate has been saved. You were sent to rescue the unsaved, and while you are doing so, in your obedience, your mate will present himself or herself to you. Your mate won't be the person who you pull up or coach; your mate will be the person alongside you trying to help someone else to safety. Your mate is found in your obedience to God, and won't be found anywhere else. We are often drawn to people who need the most help, nevertheless, we are simply not strong enough to pull them up because the pull of sin is so great that God sent Jesus to save them.

I've been guilty of looking at the exterior of a man and thinking that his rebellion was actually his strength. When I should have been helping someone up (ministering), I was trying to save men I felt would look great on my arms if they only got saved. What a treat that would be if they would realize how I went into rebellion to rescue them. Oh, how wonderful would it be to hear them tell the world how I stood by their side and helped them when they were in their weakest hour pretending to be strong. You can't save someone who refuses to grab onto God's unchanging hand because you are not God. Your spouse will be found in the Lord and never in your sin. Everyone who cries Lord, Lord isn't saved, and some will never be saved.

Know this: You can never do for a man or a woman what they refuse to do for themselves. At the same time, only JEHOVAH is God. You can only be you, but the wrong person will bring out the worst in you when God is trying to get the best out of you. That's why He requires that you wait on Him.

Marrying the Unsaved

I'm on social media sites a lot because I'm always ministering, marketing or just browsing. Because I spend quite a bit of time on social media sites, I've seen my fair share of silliness. As a matter of fact, I was on Facebook recently, and I was scrolling down my timeline when I saw a video posted up from a girl on my friends' list. I clicked the video and the girl was going off about how pathetic men are. She went on to speak directly to "the men" about their philandering ways and their inabilities to keep a good woman. To my surprise, she was a woman of faith. I could tell she'd been recently hurt and she wanted to get a message across to the man who had hurt her, as well as every other worldly man who dared to listen to her rant.

As I continued down my timeline, I came across another post, and in that post, another believing woman was ridiculing men. She was talking about how men could have a good woman at home, and mess it up for some loose woman out in the streets.

At that moment, I noticed a trend amongst many believing women— a trend that I'd once been a part of. Who were they talking to? They were talking to worldly men, trying to convince them that their two-timing ways were going to cost them good women. Now, these men have a choice between serving God and serving the enemy, and they've already chosen the latter. Why is it that so many women believe that a man could reject God and still be good to them? Why is it that so many women are trying to teach men how to be men of God? It's simple— many believing women aren't waiting on God for their spouses. They are practicing the world's way of dating and that's why they keep ending up with the world's results. God told us to not be unequally yoked with unbelievers, yet, many believing women are still testing Him by marrying unbelievers and then complaining when they act like unbelievers.

After witnessing the video and the status, I immediately recalled my two marriages and laughed. I was once like those women. I used to sit up for hours trying to come up with the best speech and the best approach to get my exes to change their ways. There were many days and nights when I had grand speeches all thought out, and I delivered those speeches to *perfection*. After my long and heartfelt speeches were over, I would sit in front of my exes, hoping that they would renounce their wicked ways, hug me, and we would reconcile. In other words, I wanted them to do for me what they would not do for God. It's funny now when I look back because I had imagined those conversations going a lot better than they did.

After thinking of what I was going to say for hours, I'd go into whatever room my husband was in, and I'd say those words most men hate to hear: *Can we talk?* I knew the first few seconds were crucial, because asking a man to talk often puts him on the offensive, so I would hurry up and make it known that I wanted peace. The tears in my eyes would drop as I recanted how hurt I was and how much I wanted our marriage to work. While speaking, I would notice that awful body language that signaled that my beau wasn't at all moved by my speech and was anxiously waiting for me to shut up so he could go off. I kept trying to change the mood before he spoke, but it didn't work. Of course, both guys had their own ways of delivery, but in both cases, the message was clear— my well-thought out speech did not move them.

After seeing that my moving speech had no positive impact on my husband, I would go back into my bedroom and soak my pillow with tears. While there, the spirit of pride would begin to minister to me. Suddenly, anger would step in, and I would think to myself that I had been far too nice. Of course, it was just the enemy seducing my mind as I allowed myself to sink deeper into my emotions. Suddenly, I would be infuriated, and I would storm back into whatever room my husband was in to deliver the message from an angry place. That still didn't work.

In my attempts to save my husbands, I tried the following:

- Talking
- Reasoning
- The silent treatment
- Crying
- Begging

- Threatening
- Reading the Bible
- Quoting scriptures
- Sex
- Withholding sex
- Asking for a divorce
- Asking for a cease-fire
- Writing notes
- Cooking feasts
- Refusing to cook
- Ripping up our pictures
- Putting our pictures back together with scotch tape
- Reminding them of how good of a woman I was, and how they would never find another woman like me
- Telling stories about men of my past— men I'd dumped for far less offenses (indirect threatening)
- YouTube videos of T.D. Jakes ministering about our problem areas
- YouTube videos of Creflo Dollar ministering about our problem areas

- YouTube videos of ANYBODY ministering about our problem areas
- Talking to their family members for help
- Sending out emotional emails to his family members (second marriage) hoping to get some help
- Praying
- Fasting
- Anointing his head with oil while he slept (second marriage)
- Jumping on prayer lines
- Refusing to go back on any prayer lines
- Approaching the altar during altar call
- Speaking in tongues
- Packing my bags
- Unpacking my bags
- Leaving for a few hours
- Leaving for a few days
- Letting other religions into our home (first marriage) to minister to him—*I*

wanted somebody (anybody) to get through.

- Public flattery
- Public humiliation
- And the list goes on and on

Honestly, I could write an entire book using the lists alone.

The point is— there were no words in my vocabulary that would reach deep enough into their hearts and change their minds. Only the Word of God will transform a man's mind! **You cannot teach a man how to be a man, and you cannot reach a man who refuses to grab onto God's unchanging hand!** Instead of helping them find the good in themselves, they ended up helping me to see the bad that was in me.

Every word in the English language did not suffice. My second husband spoke five languages, and there weren't enough words in any of those languages to reach him. He needed the Word of God, not the words of Tiffany.

As I looked at my timeline once again, I considered reviewing the video of the girl ranting, but I chose not to. I thought to myself that she would probably have to walk that same path that I took just to understand that she was wasting her words. Her mind needed to be changed so she could stop desiring the type of men who were hurting her. She wanted worldly men because she was still worldly herself. She wanted a worldly man who would love her enough that he would repent to her and serve every need she had. Like many believers, she didn't understand that as a believer, she was scheduled to change. You see, once we get saved, our spirits are instantly changed, but our minds still need renovation. It takes time to change the mind, but in the meantime, we should always seek to get closer to the Father. Any woman who is still attracted to worldly men is in herself worldly, or she's still a babe in Christ. I was young in the faith when I got married both times, but I really grew up in my second marriage. In my second marriage, God matured me as I continued to feed on His Word. A few years into that marriage, I was arguing less and loving more. I then began to hear from the Lord more as to how I was to treat my husband. I had to understand that he was a man who wasn't saved and he did not see life, choices, faith or marriage the same way I saw them. But as I grew up, I began to realize that I didn't possess the words to change him. All I could do was be a light to him, and I made it a personal mission of mine to win his soul for the kingdom of God. Every time he talked about God, I found a glimmer of hope, but it would always be snuffed out a few sentences later. The issue wasn't that they (my exes) were horrible men; the issue was that I had gone

into sin, came out with sinners, and then
tried to change them. The issue was that I
was far too young spiritually to get married
when I did. The issue was that I didn't wait
on God for my husband; instead, I chose to
give me what I wanted first and then, I
tried to give God what He required later. I
found out the hard way that God has to
come first always, otherwise, it's just not
going to work.

Please understand that you can't change a
man. You'll put in many years of work,
only to find that you've wasted your time
trying to play God. At the same time, you
would have been unfair to someone who
needed salvation, but didn't get the chance
to pursue salvation at their own pace.
Instead, they married a believing woman
and she started railroading them towards
Christianity. When or if you witness this
firsthand, you'll see how unfair it is to the
unbeliever. I had a chance to choose Christ

on my own, and I approached Him at my own pace, but when I married unbelievers, I didn't give them a chance to do the same. Instead, they had to live with a woman who was trying to be the wife, the pastor, the judge, the executioner, the witness, the private investigator, and so on. Just like you were given the grace to give your heart to the Lord, other unbelievers need that same measure of grace to give their hearts to the Lord. But if you marry an unbeliever, you're not going to want them to pace it, especially when you realize that they are letting devils in and you keep having to kick those devils back out. It reminds me of when I was young and growing up in Mississippi. My siblings and I would keep going in and out of the house while my mother would be shouting for us to stay in or stay out. She would remind us that we were letting flies in. Whenever we sat down to eat, if two or more flies were swarming around us, my mother would get agitated and tell us that the flies came in when we kept opening the door to go outside or come back inside. She would then proceed to grab the fly swat and stalk the flies until she killed them off one by one. This is what we do when we're married to unbelievers. We keep telling them about the spirits they let in when they listen to demonic music, hang around ungodly characters, hang out in seedy places, etc. We then proceed to go after the spirits they've let in, all the while, telling them that they are responsible for whatever we're going through. This is why we should not marry unbelievers.

Stop trying to go after unbelievers with the intent of marrying them. You need to stay hidden in the Lord until your husband finds you. God won't just send you anyone; He'll send you a spouse after His own heart. He'll send you a spouse who will already be saved and know His voice—

someone who won't follow the voice of a stranger. He'll send you someone who fears Him— someone who seeks Him for answers. You can't resurrect a dead man; only God can. Don't try to play God in anyone's life. Let God get the glory from your marriage. After all, marriage is a God-ordained institution that mirrors our relationship with God. Do you really want to date, court or marry someone whose god is the Devil himself? Remember, marriage will always reflect our relationship with JEHOVAH (our God) and our relationship (or lack thereof) with Satan. If your spouse is a child of the Devil, you're going to get tired of those daily visits from your father-in-law. An unsaved spouse will stand against you as you stand for God. The worst thing you can do to yourself is marry the wrong person and give the enemy full-time access to your soul (mind, will and emotions) through a soul tie, full-time access to your living quarters through your spouse, full-time access to your children through the divide in your home and full-time access to your finances through your marriage. That's when you can really say you're sleeping with the enemy.

Delaying Your Husband's Arrival

It goes without saying— most people who are waiting for their God-ordained spouses are looking forward to the day that they meet them, and especially looking forward to their wedding day. The wait itself can be rather challenging, nevertheless, most challenges that singles face are self-inflicted.

I've come across many women who've said to me that they were worried that they'd have to wait five or more years for their spouses to arrive. They've seen some single and waiting leaders proclaim how they were abstinent and waiting for years, and some even waited decades. Because of this, many singles prefer to date than to wait.

But there are several reasons why some women may have waited so long for their spouses. They include but are not limited to:

1. **Rebellion:** Many people enter some form of rebellion and it takes them years to come out of. Please understand that any form of rebellion is a hindrance. Staying pure in body, but having an impure mind is still rebellion. Please know that some of the people who've waited struggled with masturbation, porn, trying to find their own spouses, bad associations, participating in worldliness and the list goes on. Waiting on God for your spouse requires much more than being abstinent. You must also remain holy.

2. **Unsevered Soul Ties:** If you've had sex, you've been married. Because most people don't look to the

scriptures in relation to just what sex is and what sex does, most people don't realize that they are still married to someone or several someones. They call Heaven and request that Heaven releases their spouses to them, but what God sees is a married woman or a married man asking for another partner. You have to repent of the past, and ask the Lord to divorce those unions.

3. **Dating, Not Waiting:** Dating is a worldly concept where a woman is taken out by any random man, and the couple spends time together getting to know each other. Eventually, the couple begins to make their rounds (first base, second base and third base). The relationship continues until one or both parties decide that they no longer want to be in that relationship. It's easy to see why God

is against this practice. As believers, we have to understand that we are people of purpose, and this means that our relationships should also have purpose. We shouldn't involve ourselves in the worldly practice of dating. Instead, we must remain prayerful in everything and get God's confirmation in all things.

4. **Unforgiveness:** A lot of women don't realize this, but anytime you operate in unforgiveness towards another person, you are pretty much still soul-tied to that person. You're that person's slave, or at minimum, you are a slave to your hatred. I'm not sure why some women truly believe that holding onto unforgiveness is going to somehow reward them someday when it is not. An unforgiving heart is a dark heart that's constantly being attacked by Satan. It drains the life out of people

and affects their health. It is always better to forgive those who've hurt you than it is to stay joined to them in anger.

5. **Making Marriage an Idol:** Some women are absolutely obsessed with the idea of getting married to the point where they are following every leader who preaches about marriage. They are taking notes, following rules, attending conferences and just overly obsessing over the idea of getting married. Here's the thing—it's great to follow and learn from those who have waited and reaped their special someones, but you also need to remember that God is a jealous God. Sometimes, I don't think people really understand how jealous He is. You simply can not place marriage before God; that's not even an option. How do you know if marriage is an idol for you? It's

simple— if you study being married more than you study being in right standing with God, marriage is an idol, and you need to repent. Seek the kingdom of Heaven and all its righteousness first and foremost, and let God worry about the marriage part.

6. **Monitoring Their Biological Clocks:** God holds time in His hands, so it's pretty offensive to Him when we try to imply that He can only do certain things during certain times in our lives. For example, most women have children between the ages of 18-30. The closer a woman gets to the thirty year age mark, the more anxious she becomes to get married. After all, she has to deal with wondering if she'll ever have kids, pestering questions from her relatives, concerned peers and not being able to relate to most of her

friends who happen to have children.
Men, on the other hand, don't worry
about their biological clocks so much
because men usually remain fertile
for the rest of their lives. We can't
rush God; we can only trust that He
will do what He says He will do in
His time and not ours.

7. **Becoming Stagnant:** A lot of women
   think that they are just to remain as
   they are, and their husbands will
   come along and rescue them.
   Because of these mindsets, they end
   up waiting for years— sometimes,
   decades. We are creatures of
   purpose, help meets and vessels of
   honor. In order for our husbands to
   find us, we need to be operating in
   our purpose, and we need a better
   understanding of what it means to be
   help meets.

8. **Jealousy:** I can't tell you how many
   women I've met who've battled with

jealousy. It's not uncommon for women to reach out to me and complain about some woman who's fornicated her way into marriage. Instead of realizing that the Word of God is true and that God won't bless such a union, the women call God unfair in so many words. This is jealousy and jealousy is a spirit that comes in when we lack knowledge and understanding. That's why we need to pursue them both. Jealousy will hold back a woman from being found, because you have to understand that if she is jealous of people who've sinned their way into marriage, she's going to be a jealous wife. This means that her husband will have to be extremely careful in his dealings with other women. Now, it's a given— every single and married man should exercise wisdom when dealing with members of the opposite sex, but for a jealous woman, her husband's decision to greet a female co-worker could turn into a war.

9. **Blaming Others (including God) and Not Self:** I've been married twice, and both times, I sinned my way in. Because of my sins, my marriages were ungodly institutions where I felt imprisoned, remorseful and repeatedly hurt. Both of those marriages ended in divorce, but do I have the right to blame God for not letting me keep the fruit of my sins? No way! And I wouldn't be foolish enough to launch a complaint against Him. The sin was my own, and I have no one else to blame for what happened but myself. I couldn't even blame the men because I knew they weren't saved when I married them. Any woman who does not take the blame for her own errors is a

woman who is not ready to be a wife. After all, marriage is not a union for two perfect people; it's a union where two imperfect people will join themselves as one person and attempt to stay joined. A woman who does not recognize the error of her ways will always deflect her errors onto her husband, and by doing so, she will constantly divide her own home.

10. **Being anxious:** Many souls want to be married, but don't know or understand that being anxious is a work of the flesh. You can't rush God, but you can slow down the reception of your blessings by getting anxious.

11. **They picked a mindset and stayed there for too long:** God wants to renew our minds, but we have to be willing in order for this process to begin and complete itself. A lot of

believers are still operating in the same mindsets that they had before they got married. Understand this— God told us to be changed by the renewing of our minds; this is a command. He didn't say that by getting saved, we'd automatically pick up new mindsets. God won't send a godly man to a woman who has worldly thinking.

12. **They want the wedding more than they want the marriage:** Some women want the wedding more than they want to be married. There are many women out there who have dreamed of their wedding days ever since they were children. If you talk to them about marriage, they'll go on and on about their elaborate plans for their weddings, but they have little to no plans for the actual marriage. Until their minds change, they won't be found by their God-

appointed spouses.

13. **Using abstinence as a tool and not a sacrifice:** I've seen this countless times. A woman announces that she's proudly standing her ground against her "boyfriend's" advances. Listening to her speak reveals that her love interest is indeed worldly and likely unsaved. She goes on to minister to other single women because <u>she's proud of herself</u>. Another month has gone by in her three-month long relationship, and she still hasn't given in yet. Now, (in her mind) she's well on her way to a double-altar call: marriage and then getting Paco delivered, or better— getting Paco delivered and then marriage (*whichever one comes first*). And how did she accomplish this feat? By withholding sex from an unsaved man. Now, if you've ever been in the world or known a person

who's unsaved, one thing you'll
know is that most unsaved men
aren't faithful. They aren't in the
faith, so they don't have the faith to
be faithful. Most of them have
several sex partners. But somehow,
like many women, she's come to
believe that by closing her legs, Paco
will open his heart to Jesus. You
cannot manipulate God!
Additionally, choosing to remain
abstinent, and then, choosing to
disobey God by marrying an
unsaved man is still disobedience.
Either way, you did not do what God
said and you will reap of whatever it
is that you have sown.

14. **Evil communications:** Let's say that
    God told you that He was going to
    bless you with a million dollars, but
    in order to receive that million
    dollars, you must be standing in a
    certain place. You stand there, but

you keep watching the clock because
your best friend wants you to pick
her up at four o'clock that evening
and hang out with her for a few
hours. After standing in place for
several hours and receiving
numerous calls from your best
friend, you decide to go and pick her
up, hang out with her for a few and
then get back in place to wait for
your million dollar transfer. You pick
up your friend, and the two of you
have a great time. After you hang out
with her, you take her home and
return to the spot that you were
supposed to be waiting. You see
several money bags on the ground,
but they are all empty. It turns out
that the money came, but your
enemy used your friend to distract
you while he robbed you. That's
what evil communications is. It is a
distraction. Many men and women

have delayed their waits because
they refuse to let go of the
relationships that God has told them
to let go of. Because of this, they are
not in position to be found.

Some people teach that a woman can
shorten her wait by performing a bunch of
works. This is not true! Truthfully, such
teaching borders on witchcraft. With God,
there is a season for everything and this
means that we can't shorten our waits, but
we can delay them. How so? By sinning
against God or doubting Him. When we
doubt God, we'll easily date any man who
looks like he has the potential to be our
husbands. The greatest test of a waiting
woman is a man who could easily end her
wait and give her everything she's been
wanting in a husband. Believe it or not,
those guys will come, and in most cases,
they are tests. Sadly enough, most women
fail their tests by marrying them or

entering into sexual immorality with them. Of course, this delays the God-appointed husband's arrival— sometimes by several years.

There are many things that we can do to delay our spouses' arrival, but if we follow God and if we obey Him, we won't have to worry about our husbands being delayed. Delays usually happen to the rebellious, the backslidden and those who lack understanding. Nevertheless, a woman who fears the Lord and refuses to let Satan entertain her flesh is a woman whose husband is right on time, even if he hasn't arrived yet.

Wisdom for the Wait

When a little girl is born, her father knows that he needs to protect her. He sees the beautiful little creature that she is and he knows that she is depending on him for protection. She is weak, helpless and at the complete mercy of her parents. Many fathers look at their precious newborn daughters and vow to protect them all the days of their lives. There is something about the weakness in a woman, especially a tiny woman, that wakes up the protector in a man. At the same time, having a daughter sometimes helps husbands to realize the vulnerability and softness their wives possess. Many men have reported that they've become better husbands after having daughters.

As the little girl gets older, the father's

desire to protect her continues to strengthen, especially when the innocence of her youth can be heard in her many words. This doesn't change when she turns sixteen years old, which, of course, is the age that many Americans allow their daughters to start dating. Most fathers oppose the idea of their daughters dating, but they oftentimes give into the pressures from their wives. Even though their daughters may look like women to others, the fathers still see their little girls. More than that, they can still hear that youthful ignorance in their daughter's words. She needs to be protected from the crafty wolves who would easily take advantage of her, and many fathers know this.

Many parents send their teenage daughters out on dates, but when those girls return, they are no longer virgins. *NBCNews.com* reports the following: The average male loses his virginity at age 16.9; females

average slightly older, at 17.4. Of course,
when a young woman loses her virginity,
she loses a big part of herself. This only
aids in making her emotionally unstable
and unable to focus on school and her
future. Somehow, a father knows this and
he does everything in his power to protect
his little girl, but if his wife is not siding
with him, he agrees to send his little girl
out, hoping that what he's instilled in her
will be enough to keep her from making a
bad choice. This is very similar to how God
is with His daughters.

When we are born again, we start off as
babes in Christ; we are like infants and God
knows that we need His protection more
than anything. As we grow up in the Lord,
our innocence and our ignorance can be
heard in our words, especially when we
think we've got Christianity and God all
figured out. He wants to protect us from
the many wolves who would take

advantage of us, but when we think we are ready to be wives, we'll oftentimes rebel against God. Just like a teenage girl turns to her mother for help, we will turn to religion to justify our desires to have relationships with the guys we've chosen for ourselves. We tell ourselves that we can win these guys to the Lord, they aren't as bad as others make them out to be, and the most common excuse for going after an ungodly man is, "God knows my heart." Being a gentle and loving Father, the Lord allows us to exercise our own free will, even though He knows that the men we've chosen for ourselves are rebels. Sadly enough, He has to watch as His daughters are returned to Him one after the other, and most of them are no longer virgins. He then has to do like a natural father and try to restore His daughters with kind words and careful rebukes. To make matters worse, we then behave like teenagers and we blame our Father for the ending of our relationships. Why did He interfere or why didn't He interfere? Why didn't He talk with the guys we had chosen for ourselves? Why didn't He support our relationships? Our emotionally charged rants only serve to validate the fact that we are not yet ready to be wives.

God continues to protect us, but when we're young in the faith and determined to get what we want when we want it, we continue to rebel against Him. He watches time after time as we go out and defile ourselves with sin and then, we return to Him broken, angry and confused. We want to be wives and mothers, but God wants us to stop and just be His daughters. He will send our God-appointed husbands to us in due season, but we have to trust Him when He says that we are not yet ready.

I worked in retail for seven years and I remember seeing little boys and girls throwing tantrums whenever their parents refused to buy something for them. I would shake my head in disgust as the parents would try to reason with their children, instead of taking control of the situation and letting those children know that their behaviors would not be tolerated. I was even more disgusted by the parents who would give in and give their children whatever it was they were crying for. I thought of my own mother, laughing at the realization that I had never pulled that stunt with her because she wasn't afraid of going to jail. I'd even witnessed her whooping my little sister in the checkout lane after she'd tried the "fall down and scream" stunt because my mother refused to let her get some M&M's. There was even an incident when my sister had stolen a pack of M&M's after my mother refused to get them for her. Of course, my mom found the candy, took my sister back to the store and made her return it. After that, she disciplined her for the theft.

As much as I shook my head at those parents, I had to realize that I had pulled the same stunt with God many times. I picked up guys whom He told me I could not have. I begged for Him to approve of the relationships I wanted, but He would not. I then got crafty, went out and married the wrong men without His consent and then, tried to get Him to sign off on those marriages. He would not. Instead, He took me back to the place of my offense, and I had to release those husbands. Now, He could have given me the guys I wanted, but thankfully, He did not. Why is this? Think about the parents who give in to their children's tantrums. Without realizing it, they are pretty much giving up on their children. They've decided that their children's tantrums are just some of the not-so-nice parts of their personalities and they end up feeding those mindsets. Later on in life, many of those children end up being written-off as mentally ill or having some type of emotional disorder when, in truth, their parents should have stood their grounds with them and disciplined them. Understand this— the root word of discipline is disciple. God makes disciples out of us by disciplining us. If He was to give us what we wanted, we would be hell bound to this day. Why is this? Because there would be no reason for us to pursue renewed minds. I pursued a renewed mind after my old one kept failing me, and I was being introduced to a new way of thinking through Bible studies. When you give in to a child's tantrums, you hand that child over to a mindset of entitlement. If that child grows into that mindset, he or she won't be a very stable adult and we've all seen this happen.

Romans 1:28-32 (NIV): "Furthermore, just as they did not think it worthwhile to retain the knowledge of God, so God gave them over to a depraved mind, so that they do what ought not to be done. They have become filled with every kind of wickedness, evil, greed and depravity. They are full of envy, murder, strife, deceit, and malice. They are gossips, slanderers, God-haters, insolent, arrogant and boastful; they invent ways of doing evil; they disobey their parents; they have no understanding, no fidelity, no love, no mercy. Although they know God's righteous decree that those who do such things deserve death, they not only continue to do these very things but also approve of those who practice them."

When God told us no, He was protecting us. When He refused to give in to our many tears and pleas, He was retaining us for Himself. He could have given us over to whatever it was or whomever it was we were asking for, but because He loved us, He stood His ground. His no would echo across the hands of time until those relationships finally gave way and we realized that we could not force God to bow down to our dark desires or tantrums. When He said no, we had to live with it. When He says, "not yet," we have to wait for it. When He says, "never," we have to get over it. One thing you will never hear God say is, "I'll think about it." He is God. He is all-knowing, and He does not have a double mind.

An old friend of mine (we'll call her Danielle) was getting ready to move to another state and marry her long time boyfriend. She was preparing to quit her job and start her new life as a wife. Danielle worked with me in retail and she was more than excited to marry her guy; after all, they had a child together and she was pregnant with their second child.

There was an older woman working with

us who I'll refer to as Mrs. Banks. Mrs. Banks was a beautiful, God-fearing woman who could never seem to have a bad day. She would always hug us when she saw us and she would encourage us anytime we were down. She was almost like a second mother to us, even though we didn't know her outside of work. We were wild girls, but we respected, loved, and honored Mrs. Banks.

One day, Mrs. Banks approached Danielle and told her about a dream she had. In the dream, Danielle had been presented with two roads, but she was about to take the wrong one. Now, up until this point, Danielle had never questioned Mrs. Banks. She followed every piece of advice that Mrs. Banks had given her, but when Mrs. Banks told her not to marry the guy she was about to marry, she became offended. Hurt, she reached out to a few more older women, and they all told her what she wanted to hear. I will never forget when she approached me and told me that one of the women had said to her that the Devil could speak through anyone— including a God-fearing woman like Mrs. Banks. I was extremely mad at Danielle at this point. For me, I knew marrying the guy she was about to marry would prove to be a big mistake and I knew that it was her mistake to make, but I didn't like that she was turning on the people who did not support her decision. Mrs. Banks wasn't the only one to warn her and everyone who dared to challenge her decision was written off as her enemy.

Danielle quit her job, married her beau, and moved to another state with him. It wasn't long before she realized that Mrs. Banks was right. Her husband took her through so much heartache and pain that by the time their marriage ended, she was completely broken. Truthfully, it took her many years to recover from that marriage. Of course, she revisited her conversation with Mrs. Banks and she changed her mind about the woman of God. Over the years, anytime we talked about how she turned on everyone who told her not to marry her beau, we'd laugh and she'd tell me how crazy she was about the guy. He had been an idol to her. This makes me think of how we are with God whenever He says no to us. We turn on Him, stop speaking to Him or we'll stop speaking to Him about certain matters, and we'll go off and do whatever it is that He has told us not to do. When those situations don't pan out for us, we are forced to revisit God's warnings, and it is then that we realize that He did do as He said He would do— He opened up a way of escape for us, but we refused to take it.

I can truthfully and humbly say that I am glad that my sins did not pan out for me. I'm happy those marriages I'd put myself in did not work because they served to teach me a valuable lesson. That lesson is— the Word of God is true. It was those marriages that served to confirm the Word in my heart and they helped me to finally accept the renewed mind God was trying to give me. Those marriages drove me closer to my first love: YAHWEH. It was those marriages that served as the launching pads needed to propel me into my destiny. After my sister had stolen the candy from the store and my mother humiliated her by making her bring it back and apologize, my sister was too afraid to steal anything else. The same went for me. When those marriages did not work and my Father allowed the humiliation of those failed marriages to overtake me, I finally repented to Him and committed to never sinning against Him with my body again. I can't give me away because I don't belong to me. Only my Father in Heaven can give me away because I am His and I know this now.

You're waiting on your God-appointed husband and that's a good thing, but you need to understand that God is protecting you. He loves you so much that He doesn't want you to end up in the hands of the wrong man. He knows what He's placed on the inside of you. He knows that many of the men you would choose for yourself would take that beautiful heart of yours and break it time and time again. He would then have to convince you to bring that broken heart to Him so He could put it back together again. Convincing you that you need deliverance and restoration would be no easy task because wherever pain sets in, pride steps in. You've got to trust Him in order to obey Him. In order to trust Him, you have to know Him intimately and not just casually. I will tell any woman who wants to hear that the Word is true; you can't get around it. You have to do things God's way, and I know it isn't easy to wait for a man when you don't know how long it'll be before he arrives. But what you do need to know is that God knows when you're ready to be a wife and He knows when the man He has assigned you to is ready to be a husband. He won't release that man to find you if his mind hasn't been saved or his mind hasn't been renewed. That's why it's a good idea for you to start praying for your God-appointed husband. Ask the Lord to protect him, lead him in Christ Jesus and cancel every assignment, plot, plan, and scheme that the enemy has devised against him. Also, ask the Lord to drive away the immoral women, including the Jezebels and the Delilahs that Satan sends after him. Understand that some women will stay in God's will and refuse to entertain ungodly men and men who aren't their God-appointed husbands. Then again, some women will entertain any men they feel is

worth their time. These women are similar
to the foolish virgins that Matthews 25:1-13
speaks of.

Matthew 25:1-13 (ESV): "Then the
kingdom of heaven will be like ten virgins
who took their lamps and went to meet the
bridegroom. Five of them were foolish, and
five were wise. For when the foolish took
their lamps, they took no oil with them, but
the wise took flasks of oil with their lamps.
As the bridegroom was delayed, they all
became drowsy and slept. But at midnight
there was a cry, 'Here is the bridegroom!
Come out to meet him.' Then all those
virgins rose and trimmed their lamps. And
the foolish said to the wise, 'Give us some
of your oil, for our lamps are going out.'
But the wise answered, saying, 'Since there
will not be enough for us and for you, go
rather to the dealers and buy for
yourselves.' And while they were going to
buy, the bridegroom came, and those who
were ready went in with him to the

marriage feast, and the door was shut. Afterward the other virgins came also, saying, 'Lord, lord, open to us.' But he answered, 'Truly, I say to you, I do not know you.' Watch therefore, for you know neither the day nor the hour."

We are eternal creatures living in the laws of the seasons. Whatever we sow, we will reap. We've got to understand that we cannot sow sin and expect to reap blessings. That's like expecting a cat to give birth to a puppy. Utilize this season to get closer to God. Spend time with Him and ask Him to fill you with His precious Holy Spirit. Understand that in the beginning, it will be hard to sit still and focus on a God whom you cannot see, but you'll adjust over time if you do not give in. Let Him be your everything so that He can restore you, ripen you with wisdom and hide you in His perfect will. A wife who's hidden is a wife who can be found. A woman who's not hidden is a woman who is lost. Wait for the God-appointed husband. He will arrive in due season if you do not give up on God.

Lastly, don't pay attention to the world and its results. The world has what I like to refer to as "microwave blessings" and "mirages." They look like their sins are panning out for them and they look like they are being blessed, but this isn't true. God is simply giving them the space to repent; this is the same thing He did with both you and me. Nevertheless, their sins won't pan out for them either. Everything seems to come quickly for the world, but I can attest to the fact that anything that comes quickly isn't always worth having.

Utilize this time to prepare to be a help meet and not just some man's wife. During my wait, here are a few things that I have learned to do:

   1. I've become more organized. I've

always kept a clean house, but I'm even more organized now than I was some years ago.

2. I've targeted every unpaid bill that I saw on my credit report and paid them off.

3. I practice paying off my monthly utility bills the very minute I receive them.

4. I educated myself about credit, and now, I stay away from credit cards and debt as a whole.

5. I buy in bulk. When I go to the store, I don't buy small packs of paper towels, toilet paper or any supplies. I buy in bulk.

6. I've cut my bills in half by getting rid of cable, telephone bills, and car notes. I purchased an inexpensive car and I pay my insurance off six months at a time.

7. I've learned to cook more dishes.

8. I go out to eat at least once a week. I

don't spend time in the house waiting on some man to come along and ask me out on a date. I get up and take myself out and I spend time with the Lord. I get dressed up and I'll go to a restaurant and dine in. And I don't sit there looking lonely and pathetic either. I enjoy myself!

9. I've built more businesses and learned more trades.

10. I don't sit idly by. I work towards my dreams.

11. Lastly, but most importantly, I've grown even closer to God and He is now my everything. I will NEVER put a man in His place again. He is now the head of my life.

A few things I want to learn to do include but are not limited to:

1. Cooking other dishes. I want to be one of those women who can cook anything from scratch.

2. Become a fitness geek. Even though I'm not good at eating right or exercising now, my goal is to become health conscious and understand what's in the food I'm eating. That way, I can make wiser choices.

3. Learn another language. Even though this sounds intimidating, I passionately desire to learn one or two more languages, especially since I plan to travel more.

4. Learn to coupon. Since I buy in bulk, couponing seems perfect for me, even though I hate the idea of holding up lines.

5. Get even closer to God. What I've learned is you can never be too close to God. I want to hear His heartbeat and sense His presence daily. I don't want a religious, distant relationship with Him. I want an even more intimate relationship with Him.

This is to demonstrate that I'm not only advancing towards being a better woman, but I still have goals. I'm not focusing all of my attention on getting married; I want to be a better woman as a whole. This is what you should be doing. It may look intimidating, but it's actually really rewarding. You'd be amazed at how fulfilled you will feel when you accomplish something that does not center around having a man. Sometimes, we have to do things for ourselves; that way, we won't be flattered by the first man who does for us what we refuse to do for ourselves.

Made in the USA
Middletown, DE
05 August 2018